MUD IN THE EYE

A father and son's story of hope

Stuart and Dave Bell

New Wine Press

New Wine Ministries
PO Box 17
Chichester
West Sussex
United Kingdom
PO19 2AW

ISBN 978–1–905991–28–0

Typeset by CRB Associates, Reepham, Norfolk
Cover design by Anton Fowler, Bubble Design
Printed by Creative Print & Design, Arbertillery, UK

Contents

Dedication

To the "Miracle Maker".

Acknowledgments

Our thanks and appreciation go to the following people:

All the members of our family: Irene, Sarah, Andrew, Glen, Becki, Jermac and Trenton.

Our wider family.

David's mighty men – a faithful group of praying friends.

The members of New Life Christian Fellowship, Lincoln.

The Ground Level Team.

Our administrative support team for typing, checking and improving: Paul and Jeanie Benger, Val Seager, Sadie Hoare, Muriel Shelbourne.

Jeff Lucas and Duane White for writing the forewords.

Anton Fowler of "Bubble Design" for the book cover.

Tim Pettingale and New Wine Press for giving us an opportunity to share our story of hope.

Foreword

by Jeff Lucas

Heroes are in short supply these days. It's rare to meet someone whose life grabs you by the throat and demands your attention because of its sheer beauty. That's why most heroes are created in the minds of Hollywood producers, but exist nowhere else. They save the world, wear blue tights, have x-ray eyes and drive Aston Martins. Lara Croft may be attractive, but she's a myth. We all need heroes to inspire us, to show us that life really can be lived epically even when the sun seems to have been eclipsed.

And we need heroes who live next door. I never fail to draw breath when I hear yet another story about the late great Mother Theresa, but there's such a gap between me and her. I'm about three foot taller, slightly less wrinkly than she was, and have never been a nun. Her stunning life moves me, but I can't hear about her without being mindful of the gap. I want a hero called Fred. Or Susan. Or maybe even David.

And that's why I'm honoured to write a preface for this book. My wife Kay and I were allowed the privilege of walking (in a very limited capacity) with David Bell and his family as he battled what we all dread: the horrendous big C, the word we hate to even say: cancer. Like his Old Testament namesake, David took on his own personal Goliath with faith, humour and reality. Watching him navigate his way through his own valley of the shadow was stunning.

There were tears. There were prayers that were more like an urgent yell than a calm petition. I saw vintage love shared between the Bell family: backs against the wall, they struggled their way through those days in a hug and a huddle that was moving to see.

And I watched a young man live what he believed and prioritise what was really important. One of my own favourite memories was when David called our home in Colorado. He's done it a few times (occasionally pretending that he's Gerald Coates), but on this occasion his message was brief: "Hi, Jeff, Kay. Dave here. Just called to tell you I love you."

And that's why I commend this story to you. It's a story of a fight to the finish, of love that refused to turn to bitterness or self-centredness, and of bravery that moves me to tears even now as I tap these few words into my computer. Here you'll find faith without hype, help without slogans, and persistence without the madness that sometimes accompanies charismatic behaviour.

Foreword

by Duane White

Life is defined by moments of choice. Every person has those twists in the road when life takes you to an unexpected moment of challenge. While living and ministering in England with my family we experienced one of these "defining moments" with the Bell family.

One day life was great – new relationships were being forged, the Kingdom was advancing, there were lots of exciting and fun times serving God together. Then the next day David noticed his eye was puffy and swollen. He asked us to pray for it after dinner one night. It is funny I even remember that night, because I didn't believe it was a big deal. Little did we realize how life was handing us a major defining moment which would change all of our lives.

I will never forget when Dave and I sat in McDonald's a few days after hearing the prognosis. He momentarily threw all jokes and jests aside and forthrightly asked me, "Duane, am I going to die?" followed by, "If I live, will I lose my eye?" *How do you honestly answer a sixteen-year-old boy who has adopted you as his Godfather and has his whole future ahead of him, when you know the gravity of the facts?* I looked at him and said,

"I can't promise the outcome, but I can tell you what God's truth is, and I promise to fight with everything we have to see the truth manifested." You could see resolve and determination come into his eyes – a defining moment, as if someone had dared him to fight the massive giant who taunted his future (David never was one to back down from a dare!).

My wife, Kris, and I watched a boy who was forced to face an unexpected circumstance, become a man who stood in faith to seize the moment. As you read this book I pray you will be challenged to face the facts of your circumstance, but embrace the truth of God's promise over your life through the cross. I have heard it said, "We don't choose our moments, we only choose our response to them." Dave's story of how God healed his natural vision will inspire and challenge you to receive new spiritual eyes to see God's truth over your obstacles.

INTRODUCTION

Dave

The idea of me writing a book is extremely funny, as I have never read a book in my life, apart from the Bible of course. Having said that, I did read Jeff Lucas' book, *Lucas Out Loud* as it was dedicated to me and I thought I'd better make an effort for the lad!

I remember thinking from quite a young age that I didn't really have a story to tell or an amazing testimony of how I was freed from a major drug addiction, or how I had heroically saved someone's life. I was just an average teenager who had been brought up in a Christian home and went to church without fail every Sunday. What you are about to read over the next few chapters is unquestionably a story I did not have in mind to tell. I would not have chosen this journey and to this day still can't describe in words the fear and pain I went through. This account is unlike others as my healing did not come overnight or within a few weeks, but took well over a year. My complete healing was a combination of the outstanding skills of the medical profession and God's grace and provision. In fact, this is an exciting and hope-filled story. This book is written with absolute honesty and if you are facing major health challenges I would advise that you skip the chemotherapy and radiotherapy chapters, because I would rather you concentrate on the faith-building sections which will be far more helpful for where you are at.

I believe that I now have a perspective on life that most others don't have. I now know that each day has to be lived to the full and life needs to be lived out loud!

This book is a book of hope, for all people and for some in a hopeless situation...

Dave Bell
July 2008

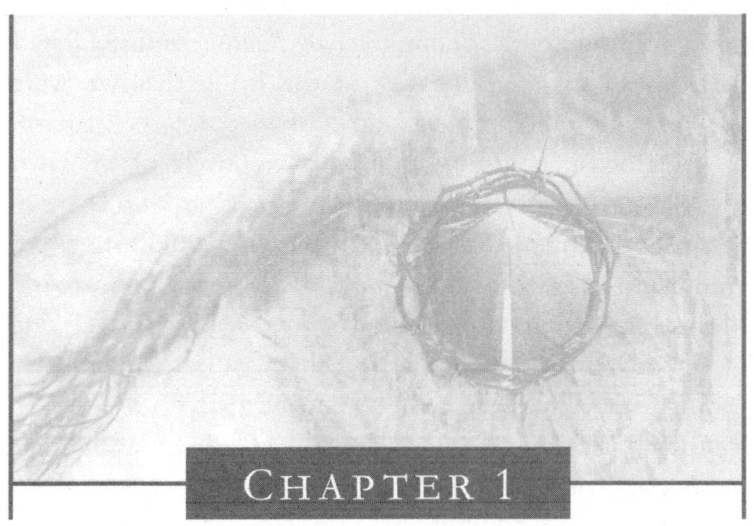

CHAPTER 1

A "NORMAL" TEENAGER

Dave

Growing up with a Dad as a church minister was sometimes a challenge. At an early age when asked by a school friend, I would somehow mistake his occupation for a policeman or a nightclub bouncer. Later on in my school years I found it a lot easier to talk about what Dad did. However, mentioning that he was a black belt in Karate would, on some occasions, creep out when I felt that it was needed.

I mentioned in the introduction about how I have never read a book. You may be wondering how I managed to pass my GCSEs and especially how I managed to achieve an "A" in English literature. There are two main reasons. First, I would always watch a DVD of the book that we were studying and not read the actual book. Second, the majority of my English course work was not entirely of my own doing. I am very fortunate to have a brother who is more academically minded than I am and I would often get Andrew to sit at the computer and "help" me with my work. Meanwhile, I would use Andrew's, let's say, "sensitive" side to my advantage by announcing that I was going to play football and that my assignment needed to be in by tomorrow morning. I'm sure that this was no great blessing to him, but for some unknown reason he would always do it!

I perhaps inherited this skill from my sister, Becki. Being the youngest child in the family didn't often have many advantages for me. However, on certain occasions it did. As Andrew and Becki were of similar ages, it would often be the two of them in disagreement rather than myself and one of them. One very funny memory of this is the time when Andrew got so mad with Becki that he resorted to giving her a quick blow to the back of the head (remember Andrew's sensitive side?!). Becki also took advantage of this by pretending that the intense clout had caused instantaneous blindness. "Andrew . . . Andrew . . . " she called out with her arms out in front of her, pretending to feel her way around. "I can't see . . . it's all gone dark!" Andrew shot out of the room like a leaping gazelle to get help as he thought that he had just blinded his sister!

Music and sport were always my two main passions throughout my school life. I was captain of the football and rugby teams and on a few occasions played football for the county. I enjoyed some parts of school, possibly all the parts there were associated with being creative but not academic.

Maths and science lessons would usually be spent on activities completely unrelated to maths or science. I had some good friendships all through my schooling and also built up good relationships with teachers.

I started playing guitar at the age of ten using a very old acoustic guitar that my Granddad gave to me. I'm pretty sure that it was crafted before the wheel, but nevertheless, it did the job. The film *Back to the Future* inspired me start playing and so the first song I learnt was *Johnny B. Goode.* Music started to take a main role in my life and at the age of twelve I began playing in a band called "Flint" with some of my close friends. We reached the heights of Nettleham Village Hall and then the village carnival, no less. Those were the days! Flint later disbanded to form the legendary "Atlas". Atlas began to play further afield and started to attract quite a following. We supported the likes of Delirious and even, on one occasion, the American superstar, Little Richard, at a big charity event.

From an early age church was a prominent element in my life. I went to church nine months before I was even born. I did go through the usual phase of wanting to play Sunday league football rather than attending church, but I am very appreciative that my parents educated me and imparted to me the importance of church life and the value of a Sunday morning. God lined up a team for me that played the majority of their matches on Sunday afternoons, so church was never compromised. I scored thirty-four goals in my first season and became a renowned striker in the league we were playing in. I was actively involved within the church worship team and connected into all youth activities.

There were three things to look forward to throughout the year in my personal calendar: Christmas, my birthday and Grapevine. Grapevine attracts up to 12,000 people annually for a Christian festival which includes worship, teaching, seminars, youth and children's activities, and live bands. Grapevine was the highlight of my year. I even think it was on a level, if not slightly better, with Christmas. I'm not suggesting that camping on a showground for five days is on a par with the birth of our Lord Jesus, but it comes pretty close!

For a long time it was apparent that I was a bit of a practical joker and on most occasions I would cross the line in one way or another. Youth weekends away would often prove this fact. On one occasion I managed to conceal around ten different alarm clocks within the youth leader's dormitory, all set with fifteen-minute intervals and starting at 3.00am. I found it really funny, but somehow I don't think she did. Another time when I attended cell group the line was crossed again. I have trouble sitting still for longer than ten minutes and I have to be active or doing something or I tend to lose concentration. So when it came to the prayer section I decided to sneak out through the front door to find a certain boy's mountain bike lying on the driveway. Me being me, I couldn't just walk past it without causing some sort of disruption to his journey home, so I decided to climb up the side of the house and put the bike on top of the roof. I walked home with a grin on my face wondering how long it would take him to find his bike – ingenious! Shortly after I arrived home I heard the phone ring. I could hear mum in the background profusely apologising for her son, once again, crossing the line.

Overall I was very content with life and rarely down. I had great relationships with family and friends and kept church a priority within my life. There was no room in my life for illness or struggle. I never really entertained the idea. I just presumed, like many would, that serious illness would not affect me. After all, I went to church, I didn't drink, I didn't smoke, I didn't do drugs . . . so what could possibly happen to me?

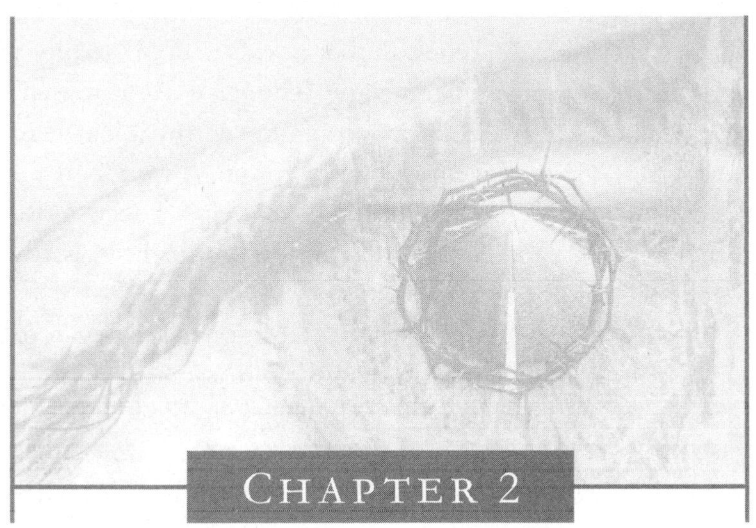

CHAPTER 2

GATHERING CLOUDS

Stuart

As a family we have always had a lot to thank the Lord for. Both Irene and I had been brought up in Christian homes and benefited from good parenting. We met one another while we were young, married, moved straight into our own home and had our first child in our early twenties. Our lives seemed kissed by grace and we would often talk together of answered prayers and God's goodness. Between 1994 and 1997 we moved into a very special season where everything around us seemed to be dusted with gold. Our family was touched by a new move of the Holy Spirit and our church began to experience renewal. I was called upon to do a considerable amount of travelling. Though I say it myself, my speaking was much improved and even my jokes were funny. One summer evening I said to Irene, "I wonder if we need to store up all this goodness to help us face more difficult days ahead." Little did I know how true these words would prove to be.

One day the page of a new chapter in our lives began to turn. Instead of blessing it seemed as though everything turned against us as an adverse wind began to blow. It began with the death of Irene's mum. We watched her slowly lose her ability to communicate as Alzheimer's disease took her away little by little. Soon afterwards my dad was taken from us, followed by my mum a few years later. Also during this period, Irene's health became a real challenge. One Monday she was admitted into hospital for a fairly routine operation. We expected that within a few days she would be on the mend, so when her blood pressure dropped and her wound refused to heal we were taken by surprise.

Irene has always been the brave one as far as hospitals are concerned, but after a few days we knew that she was really struggling. She was taken back to the operating theatre on a number of occasions and picked up a nasty infection that took months to sort out. Then one morning shortly before our annual Grapevine celebration Irene tried to get out of bed, but was so wracked with pain that we knew something serious had taken place. She had suffered with back pain for many years, but this was different. As she was determined to be at Grapevine she tried to cover up the pain, but it was obvious she would not have been able to walk. She was so determined that in the end our good friend, John Brewster, who is part of the Ground Level team, pushed her in a wheelchair throughout the event. While on site, an orthopaedic surgeon from one of our churches took her to one side and said that he would like to check her out as he was concerned that something was seriously wrong. The check-up took place in the field on an old wooden chair, but he was in no doubt that a scan was required as soon as possible. Within weeks Irene was admitted to a Sheffield hospital for major back surgery and bars and screws were fitted. The operation was successful, for which we are all very grateful. After this season of trials we assumed that we might get back to life as normal, but our greatest challenge was still to come.

David, our sixteen-year-old son, was enjoying life to the full. He was captain of his school soccer and rugby teams. Though not academic by nature, he was doing well in school and was about to face GCSE exams during the summer term. On occasions he would complain of a "sleepy eye", especially if he was extra tired. When looking in a particular direction his eye appeared to droop. Eventually he visited the doctor who thought it was likely to be an infection. Following a course of eye drops there was no improvement and he was subsequently booked in to see a consultant. The eye began to swell and he was sent for a scan. A few days later Irene received a telephone call. The scan showed a mass at the back of the right eye and David was referred to a specialist hospital in Leicester, a city over forty miles away. We were urgently passed on to a new consultant and a further scan was scheduled. At this point we still felt sure there was nothing too seriously wrong. After all, he had recently had a nasty clash of heads in a local football match, so perhaps the knock had caused some internal swelling. I have always been an expert in diagnosing family ailments. Every parent knows something about the complex issues facing children and if we worried about every ache, pain, rash or twitch we would never be worry free. So we genuinely were not expecting anything too serious. However, darker clouds were beginning to gather.

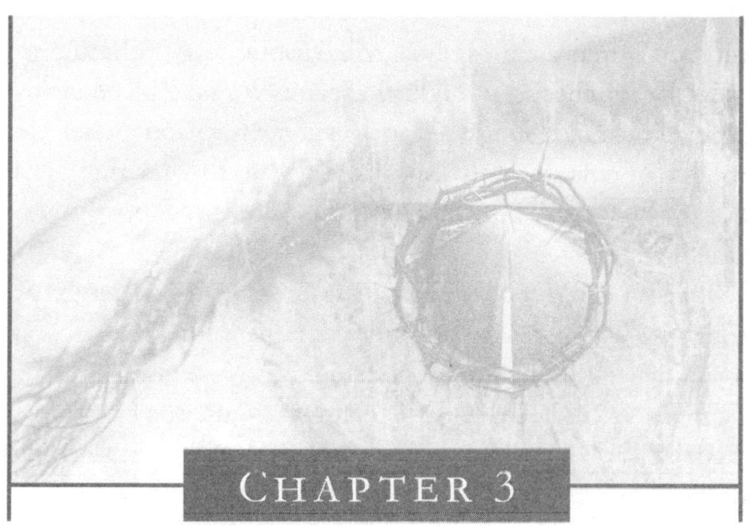

CHAPTER 3

THE LONG WEEK

Stuart and Dave

The scan revealed a growth and a biopsy was scheduled. David bravely faced the operation, but at this point none of us expected what was to follow. David returned to the ward and I was personally pleased the eye was covered as incisions and eyes are not a good combination for me. Within a very short time the surgeon, still bedecked in blue overalls and white mask, guided us into a small consultation room to share with us his findings. He kept the formalities to a minimum, but his set face told us something of the story before any words were delivered. "We managed to take more of the growth than expected but I am almost certain that it is cancer." I have tried to analyse the next few moments many times, but still find it very difficult to describe the feelings; very little seemed to take place in my brain. For me, feelings began to surge from somewhere in the pit of my stomach. My mouth was dry and my heart began to race. Then a general numbness almost overwhelmed me.

I wish I could tell you that scriptures rushed through my thinking, but in reality nothing came to mind. The closest event that comes near to describing those first few moments happened to us last week at 1.00am on Wednesday morning. Irene and I had got to bed fairly late and were soon sleeping deeply when we were awakened by the whole room shaking. We instinctively jumped out of bed, wondering whether the roof would fall in. This was of course the 5.2 earthquake which was to be the main news item the following morning. The epicentre was just up the road from us. We don't go to bed expecting earthquakes.

Just like an earthquake our world was now being shaken in an unexpected way and we were in such shock that it was going to take us some time to get our heads around the news. Imagine beginning a day expecting it to be the same as any other day when suddenly everything, in a moment of time, is being challenged. We were confused, disoriented and standing on the edge of a black hole called fear. Dave now shares his perspective after his biopsy:

> "I am starting to wake up from the biopsy to find Dad and Mum sitting round my bed holding my hand. I grumble to Dad and ask how the operation went and if it was serious. He replies in a calm voice, "The operation went well, Dave, however, the consultant has seen some things that he's not happy with." I would be

lying if I said that I'm not afraid when I hear this. However, I feel a grace come over me that leaves me feeling calm and at peace. I put in my headphones and listen to Delirious. Later on that night, after the anaesthetic has worn off, I walk to the hospital bathroom to see what my eye looks like after the operation. I am shocked to find a prominent black scar staring at me that stretches the entire length of my eyelid. It looks severely bruised and swollen. I lie back in the bed and start to think in more detail about what can be wrong with me and what the possibilities are. I have images of me having more operations and visions of the consultant removing my eye.

Later that night I start to panic and begin to cry with worry and fear. I ask Dad to call our close friends, Duane and Kris White, to see if they will drive the two hours to come and see me. Dad returns with the news that they are on their way. I count the time down until they arrive. When I see them walk in, my spirits lift. Duane prays for me and stays with me for a long time, for which I am very grateful. When it's time for him to leave, I get out of my bed and walk him to the lift. Just before the lift doors close I tell him that I never had a Godfather and nervously ask him if he will take on the role. He says yes! I feel so proud that I have Duane and Kris White as my new Godparents – now that takes some beating! The lift doors close and I walk back with a few tears in my eyes to tell Mum and Dad my exciting news . . .

These were my immediate thoughts and reactions at the time. When I left the hospital I entered the darkest week of my life – the terror of the unknown, the intense

> fear of what could be around the corner. The first night back at home I sat quietly on the end of my bed. Dad came into my room to see if I was OK. The conversation that followed I will never forget. I asked Dad some really tough questions that had been tormenting my mind ever since I walked out of the hospital doors: 'Am I going to lose my eye? . . . Will I go blind?' Not easy questions for anyone to answer, especially a father to his son. Dad replied, 'We just don't know the answers to these questions yet, Dave, but I do know God will get us through it.' I started to ask the 'why me?' questions. What had I done so wrong to deserve all of this? Is life ever going to be the same again?"

David was not the only one asking questions. Irene and Duane White were also in the room that day trying to come to terms with their feelings. Such days should not be lived alone and we were grateful for one another's combined strength. The surgeon was kind and affirming, but told us that it would take some time to find out what kind of cancer was present behind our son's eye. We nervously shook hands and we were left on our own to think through the implications. Within a few hours our good friend, Martin Dyer, who just so happened to be the professor overseeing oncology research in Leicester, assured us that he would get his team to work around the clock to find out what kind of cancer we were dealing with and that's exactly what he did. I'm so grateful that not all God's people are called primarily to the Church! Martin was a God-given gift to us at this moment of shaking. We returned to the ward to find David beginning to wake. I sat by his bedside and told him the results of the tests followed by the words, "God is with us."

As a church leader with responsibility for a growing local church and a network of churches I felt an enormous weight descend upon me. There was now a huge expectancy on me to deliver the goods and see my son healed, but this mountain seemed too high for me to climb. I grappled with the concept of being both church minister and David's dad. On occasions I felt my roles change, but primarily this was my son and as hard as it was going to be, I would have to walk through both his pain and my own. For years I had preached about the kind of faith that was now being attacked. My belief systems were being confronted by the realities that stood defiantly like giants before us. What about the sovereignty of God? What about the healing ministry in our church? Would we get our breakthrough? Alongside this sense of inadequacy, however, was a sense of strategic direction. The long week also became a week of prayer, as we will see later, but as each day blurred into the next we longed to receive some positive news.

We prayed more this week than we ever had before. Eventually the day arrived when we had to return to Leicester to receive the results of the biopsy. With stomachs churning we set off. Pete and Kath Atkins came with us (Pete is both a close friend and at the time was our GP). We tried to keep upbeat for David's sake, but the drive to the hospital was an effort. The consultant smiled and delivered the facts: "It is cancer, a rare cancer, but it is so aggressive that it is highly treatable with chemotherapy and therefore David will not require surgery to remove the tumour." We also found out that if the tumour had been benign they may have had to remove the eye. You can imagine the mixed emotions. We were being extended hope. David told me later that as a small boy he had two fears. One was that he would lose his sight and the other that he would lose his hair. At the age of sixteen he was facing both these giants, but by God's grace he was to become "David, the giant slayer". The devil is bad, but God is bigger and immeasurably better. We hugged each other with the growing understanding that God would save our day.

Our burst of joy was short lived. We were introduced to a new consultant who would take us on the next stage of our journey. This doctor of few words, who in the initial stages scared us all considerably, led us down a corridor into the children's oncology ward where small, bald-headed children with feeding tubes in their noses greeted us. Within a short period of time David was introduced to the concept of a Hickman line, a tube surgically attached to the top of the heart for the administering of chemotherapy and the taking of blood. On the journey home I was amazed that David wanted us to break the journey with a visit to McDonald's, a place not on the top of my priority list.

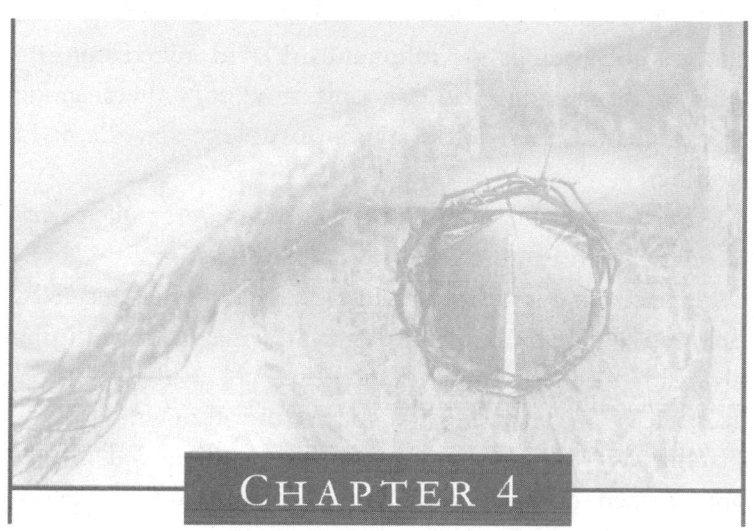

CHAPTER 4

What on Earth Should We Do?

Stuart

This was the question Irene asked as we lay side by side in three makeshift beds in the hospital ward the night after the biopsy. Perhaps I should explain that having travelled from Lincoln the night before in order to have David ready for his operation in the morning, we assumed we would find a hotel and therefore have to leave him for the night. On the way to Leicester David muttered, "I bet they give me a bed in the middle of two wizened old men." Sure enough, as David was allocated his bed, either side there they were – old and indeed wizened. I lectured him that we must begin to confess good things so, reluctantly, David joined me in a quick prayer asking God not only to change the sleeping arrangements, but also to make it possible to stay the night with him.

After a quick chat with a nurse, curtains were pulled back to reveal an area of the ward not in use and soon three beds were placed in a line for mummy Bell, daddy Bell and baby Bell. We lay side by side, our minds and imaginations flitting feverishly from one thing to the next. As David sank into a deep sleep Irene and I whispered our thoughts to one another. We exchanged our concerns and moved in and out of sleep. Somewhere in between sleep and consciousness I pondered Irene's question and as the morning broke I whispered, "I think God is giving me a strategy." As I rearranged thoughts in my mind, a pattern began to emerge. We would find a way through. We would rally prayer. We would divide the prayer times between soaking prayer and battling prayer. Then the words came clearly into my mind, "Call David's mighty men."

When I got home later I put my thoughts down on paper and to my surprise a realistic plan of action began to emerge. This was going to be our greatest challenge of faith. The start and end of our strategy must be Jesus and faith in His power to heal, but we would also recognise God's hand on the medical profession. We would pray for healing and we would cover every medical procedure in prayer also. We would try to avoid putting the spiritual in a box, believing that God is Lord over everything. We would have loved an overnight miracle, but as we set out in faith like the children of Israel, we lived with daily miracles. The battle lines were now drawn.

The treatment would soon begin, but the tumour continued to grow. David's right eye was being forced out of the eye socket causing him to hold his head back in order to see. We fought in prayer for his eye. Pete our GP came daily to check his sight. We would wait anxiously to see if things had deteriorated overnight. When we later saw the tumour on the MRI scan we were in no doubt of its source. It was hideously causing the eye to protrude and fighting for control. This image helped us to pray as we called on God to deliver David. In fact, we often pronounced the words of 1 John 3:8: *"The reason the Son of God appeared was to destroy the devil's work."* On one occasion I had to resist the enemy's taunt telling me that it is better to enter heaven with one eye than ... This quotation from Matthew 5:29 came packaged in darkness and I was reminded from the story of the temptation of Jesus that the devil is able to quote Scripture too. We declared that the eye is the light of the body.

For us, being clear about the source of the problem became very important. One morning Pete placed a book in my hands. It was a book about Smith Wigglesworth called *Wigglesworth: The Complete Story*[1] by Julian Wilson. As I opened the book it fell open at the beginning of a chapter discussing cancers. Wilson wrote, "Wigglesworth claimed that ninety percent of diseases were satanic in origin and top of the list, as far as he was concerned, was cancer. 'When you deal with a cancer case,' maintained Wigglesworth, 'recognise that it is a living, evil spirit that is destroying the body ... You must never treat a cancer case as anything else but a living, evil spirit that is destroying the body. It is one of the worst kinds of evil spirits I know. Not that the devil has anything good – every disease of the devil is bad, either to a lesser or greater degree – but this form of disease is one that you must cast out.' There were many occasions when he did just that."

To a modern-day reader this approach may seem a little extreme, but we decided that day that we would battle with everything at our disposal until the disease was defeated. Albert Hibbert in his book, *Smith Wigglesworth – The Secret of His Power*[2] wrote, "Many theologians would disagree with him but, having disagreed, could not produce the tangible evidence in support of their theories that he produced in his ministry." Friends stood with us and David seemed to be strangely submerged in God's love. His bravery was unreal at times and clearly God-given. So step-by-step we began to move forward in confidence. We put together a strategy that involved regular prayer, but also involved getting as much help as possible. After phoning Mal Fletcher he managed to contact Reinhard Bonnke's prayer team who agreed to pray.

On Irene's birthday I rang Roger and Faith Forster who said they would meet us at Stansted Airport. Roger and Faith proved to be an incredible support for us. Their son had overcome cancer against all the odds years before. As we sat over a cup of coffee it felt as though we were being drip-fed faith and confidence as they spoke with us. Roger then reached into his pocket for a small bottle of oil, which he always carries with him, and anointed David's forehead. This was the best birthday present Irene could have received that year. In fact kindness began to flow our way. On Thursday that week a Playstation was sent and on Friday a new set of golf clubs arrived. In the evening Dave was playing guitar at a youth missions event and the following day we took him to Kettering as he refused to miss a gig with Flint, a band of young, talented musicians. The next day a Ferrari arrived outside our church to take him for a drive. Irene's question was being answered. We would certainly be kept doing things and now our doing was beginning to take strategic shape

Notes

1 Wilson, Julian, *Wigglesworth: The Complete Story*, Authentic, Milton Keynes, 2002, p. 120.

2 Hibbert, Albert, *Smith Wigglesworth – The Secret of His Power*, Ben Publishing, Secunderbad, India, p. 19.

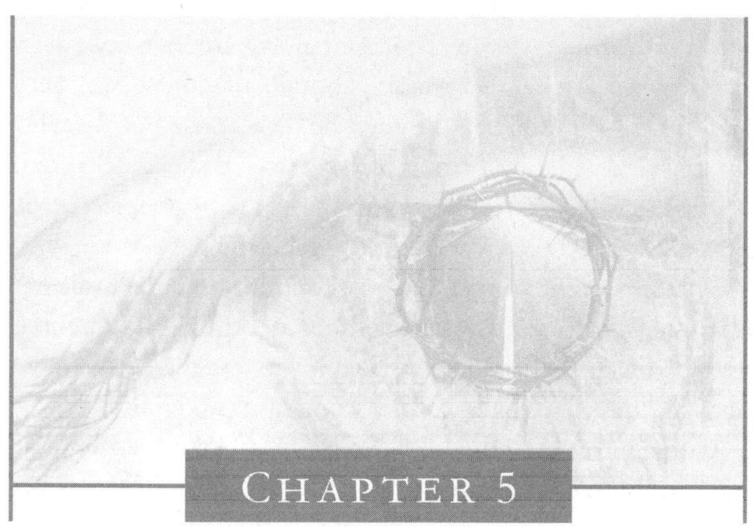

CHAPTER 5

DAVID'S MIGHTY MEN

Stuart

"Call David's mighty men." These were the words that flooded into my mind as I woke in the hospital ward. I instinctively thought of the thirty men who fought for the wellbeing of King David in the Bible. They were brave and true warriors who were determined to see breakthrough and victory. On one occasion one of the elite band broke through the battle lines at great danger to himself, just to get David a drink of water from the well of Bethlehem. These men killed lions in pits on snowy days and generally knew how to fight. So I began to call friends or prayer warriors to stand with us for total and absolute victory. I resisted giving an open invitation to the special meetings we set, though of course we were grateful for the prayers of everyone. We chose people who would stand with our focus, which was to see David delivered, set free and healed. Jesus, on occasions, kept people out of prayer meetings if they weren't on the same page as He was. The last group of people that you want around are "wailers" if you're looking for a positive outcome. I didn't want people involved who perhaps felt we were being taught a lesson, we needed a group that were of the same heart and mind.

God gave us an incredible group. I also kept members of our family free from pressure as much as possible. On the 13th of June we called the first prayer meeting at 8 o'clock. *Thirty* people arrived and as soon as we began to pray everyone engaged God with passion. The next night, again, thirty people, some of them different from the night before, turned up to pray. The group that gathered around us really did become David's mighty men. Each of them carried weight in the battle. We felt our arms were constantly being lifted up as these mighty men and women not only prayed, but also prophesied. We gave people permission to be wrong and encouraged them not to hold back. One person said they saw David as an adult standing with his own children. We believe this will happen. During "the long week" we met every night for an hour. On the sixth evening thirty arrived again. This had happened each prayer session, even though many more than thirty had been over the whole time. There was one more night to go before we returned to Leicester for the results of the biopsy, so I kept the amazing information about the numbers until the final evening. Throughout the whole event I wanted to make sure that we were not pretending or imagining things.

Before the final meeting of the week I watched the door with a sense of anticipation as people gathered. By 7.30pm twenty-nine had arrived, so I decided that perhaps it had just been a coincidence on the other evenings. As I resigned myself to the possibility of this, the door opened and in walked the thirtieth. David's thirty mighty men had literally been with us for the week. Thirty had stood with us as thirty stood with King David in 2 Samuel chapter 23. By our second evening of prayer I recorded in my diary, "We felt lighter." After the critical week we began to pace ourselves for the long haul. We met every Sunday evening and committed to keep praying together until we experienced the breakthrough. Some evenings we had soaking prayer where we gently prayed and affirmed God's promises. On other nights we had battle nights where we aggressively addressed the cancer in the name of Jesus. David said he preferred the battle nights. We learnt as we prayed and for some this became the most powerful meeting of the week. The more we prayed, the bolder we became.

Week after week scripture was declared over David concerning his future. We pronounced that he would not lose his sight. People regularly read extracts from Psalm 91, often verses 5–7 were quoted:

"You will not fear the terror of night,
nor the arrow that flies by day,
nor the pestilence that stalks in the darkness,
nor the plague that destroys at midday.
A thousand may fall at your side,
ten thousand at your right hand,
but it will not come near you."

New levels of confidence began to grip us and increasingly we were feeling safe *"... under the shelter of the Most High."* On occasions David would say, "I feel guilty. Other people around me [on the hospital ward] are struggling with infections and I always have my treatment on time." This led us to pray for the other children regularly by name. In fact, God was giving us answers for other situations in the church. For instance, a young newly-married couple, Graeme and Charlotte, shortly after their wedding day were catapulted into the realization that Graeme had a cancer in his chest. Our prayer team were immediately ready to stand with them. God had taught us many things and with these principles in place we stood with them in their battle until they also were free.

Following one chemotherapy session David noticed that a finger on his right hand was "locking". Although compared with other things this seemed relatively small, this was his plectrum finger so playing the guitar became difficult. Playing guitar was proving to be therapeutic and, just as when King David played his harp, we noticed the darkness seemed to disperse. One Sunday evening one of our prayer team brought a verse from Psalm 144, *"Praise be to the LORD my Rock, who trains my hands for war, my fingers for battle."* We prayed for the finger and in a short time it was back to normal. We were told that chemotherapy can cause this kind of condition, but his finger was completely healed. On many occasions we declared the scriptures and in particular the Psalms became a huge source of strength to us. Everyone remained focused and we encouraged one another.

The team was made up of young and old, black and white, male and female, but loved being together and enjoyed unusual levels of unity. It was this unity, I believe, that contributed towards attracting the presence of God and His commanded blessing. We laughed together and cried together. We spoke out scripture together and stood in agreement together. Sometimes we sat David in the middle of the circle and prayed, other times we would break into groups to pray. On certain nights there was a flow of prophetic words, other nights we lingered in God's presence. We were eager to hear from God and to be directed by the Holy Spirit. We remain indebted as a family to this group of dedicated and wonderful people who not only gave of their time but of their lives also.

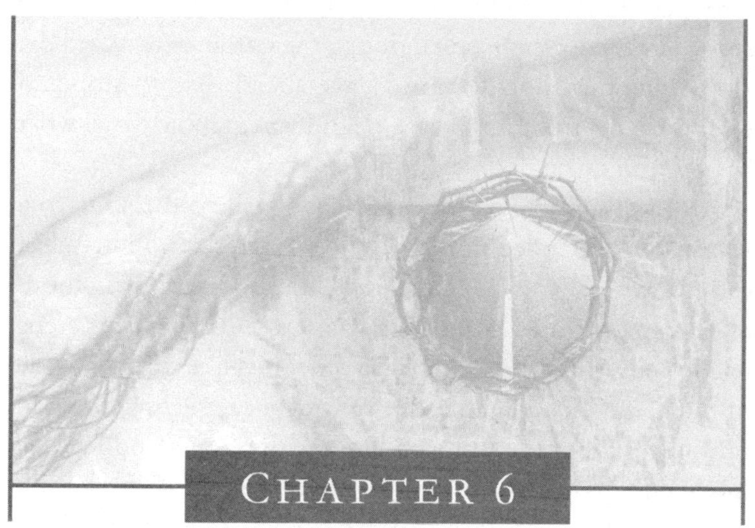

Chemotherapy

Dave

I sit here in my office quite nervous of the chapter I am about to write. I have been putting this one off, knowing that a lot of dark memories will come flooding back when I try to recollect what actually happened. Here goes . . .

After receiving the unwanted news from the consultant I am immediately rushed to meet my new oncology consultant who will explain in more detail the treatment protocols that I am to take. I get into the lift with Mum and Dad and press the button for the fourth floor. Four floors later the lift doors open and I anxiously step out. I tilt my head right back so that I can see and head towards a prominent sign saying, "Ward 27 – Children's Oncology". I go on ahead and open a set of large wooden hospital doors, the entrance to Ward 27. (In writing this short section I have already had to stop and clear the tears from my eyes, as I know in graphic detail what lies beyond those double doors.)

As I walk in it is as though I have walked through "the wardrobe" or landed in Neverland, but this is no fairytale I can just wake up from – this is real life and Ward 27 is about to become my new home. I take a few more nervous steps inside with Mum and Dad by my side. It is like watching one of the news documentaries we only ever see sittting down in our peaceful homes. Little children with no hair and feeding tubes coming out of their noses are lying in beds. I can't distinguish between life and death in some sleeping children. A friendly nurse called Rachel takes me on a brief tour of the ward. She leads me into a room where I find a little bald child sitting on the end of his bed. I stare into his eyes trying to contemplate the fact that I will be "one of them" in a matter of days. I am introduced to a doll that is fitted with a Hickman line. Rachel informs me that I will be fitted with one and this is how they will administer the chemotherapy and how they will take blood.

One week on, I return to the ward to become subject to a whole week of intense testing. Every test you can think of I have to have, all in one week. By this time my eye is at its worst stage yet and the tumour is aggressively forcing my eyeball out of its socket. Here is a list of what has to be done:

- A series of blood tests
- Kidney function tests
- MRI scans
- CAT scans

- Chest x-rays
- ECG heart test and scan
- Hearing tests
- Full body bone scan
- Visual tests and photographs taken for doctor training materials
- A visit to the sperm bank (the best test so far!)
- Neurology tests
- Lumber puncture
- Hickman line surgically fitted under general anaesthetic

Not too bad for a week's work! A few of the above procedures are, for obvious reasons, quite hard to weigh up. At the age of sixteen you don't really expect to have to think about the future in relation to having children, but I am told that the treatment might lead to me becoming infertile. As you can imagine, many sixteen-year-olds never have to hear these words, but I am one of the very few that do. I am so grateful for having such an amazing relationship with my Dad where I feel comfortable talking about most issues with him, including this one. I personally believe that even though this is a hard thing, you have to laugh in times of trial and try to find the funny side of it. So instead of going to the sperm bank all on my own, I decide to take a few pals with me to enjoy this unique experience. What am I thinking?! So, Jeff Lucas, Dad and I walk down the road indulging in a bit of laddish humour before the proceedings take place. I go off to do what is needed. Moments later I walk out into the waiting room, sample cup raised high cheering, "Victory!" A ripple of applause comes from the waiting room, well from Dad and Jeff anyway, everyone else looks rather traumatized!

Now onto a more serious note. My week of intense testing is coming to an end, however, there is still one more procedure to take place: the fitting of the Hickman line. The thought of this keeps me awake for many nights and even reduces me to tears. The contemplation of having a plastic tube inserted into the top of my heart and coming out of the left-hand side of my chest is sickening. I am informed that this might have to stay with me for a year. The time comes and it is my turn to go to theatre. I stop and ask Mum if I can just run away and believe that God will heal me, as I don't think I can face any more. We both cry and Mum tells me it would be irresponsible for us to do that, but God will be with us. I carry on walking towards the operating theatre with Mum and the nurse guiding me. I am led into the anaesthetic room where I lie on a bed and begin to cry. The anaesthetist tries to find a vein beneath all the bruising of the previous injections. Before he starts to inject the anaesthetic we ask if we can pray. Mum holds my hand and tries to pray the best she can whilst fighting back the tears. We pray that Jesus will come into the room with me and hold my hand throughout the operation as Mum will not be there. I slowly drift off into a peaceful sleep with Mum singing the words, "God is bigger than the air I breathe, this world we'll leave. And God will save the day, and all will say my glorious." I'm not sure what put me out first, the anaesthetic or Mum's singing; put it this way, neither are pleasant situations to be in!

My eyes gradually open an hour later in the recovery room. I feel a deep pain through my left-hand side. As I am wheeled back to the ward I now realize that the journey has begun and life is going to drastically change from this point on. I look down at my chest to find a long tube with two ends strapped up with some white tape. I have a brief lesson in all the procedures relating to how the line will be used and what to do in an emergency. The line is so uncomfortable and at first restricts a lot of movement. Sleeping is difficult and I am constantly nervous of catching it or of it even splitting. This is now a part of me for a long time to come and I can't see it getting any easier.

Eventually the epic day dawns and my treatment is to begin. The night previous to this is still a vivid memory for me. I nervously walk up the stairs to my room to go to bed knowing what lies ahead the following morning. Mum and Dad come into my room and sit on the end of my bed. We pray together and then I listen to a healing CD by Tony Miller just before I fall to sleep.

That daunting morning has arrived, I am not dreaming, this is real life and today is the day that I start chemotherapy. I pack my bags, my quilt and pillow and get into Dad's car. We start driving and head for Leicester. Little did I know how familiar this journey would become over the next few years. You may be wondering why I have taken my quilt and pillow. Here's the hard part: each treatment lasts for three days and the majority of this time is spent lying in a bed. An hour and thirty minutes later I arrive at the Leicester Royal Infirmary. It should have been considerably less but the Reverend was behind the wheel. I arrive on the ward and am swiftly taken to a little side room where I am going to spend the next three days. I am informed that I will be given three chemotherapy drugs throughout my stay, which were Vincristine, Ifosfamide and Actinomycin-D.

My Hickman line is then connected to an IV machine, which pumps a fluid called mesna around my body to help prevent internal bleeding and damage to my major organs.

This is injected constantly for the entire three days meaning that well over six litres of the stuff is passing through my body. Within five seconds of the mesna starting I begin to feel really sick and begin to get strange tastes in my mouth. I start to worry. If this fluid is only there to protect me, what will the chemotherapy feel like? Three hours later it is time for my first lot of treatment. I already feel sick and very weak before it even begins. A large black bag is hung up onto the machine and then connected to the spare tube on the Hickman line. (Before I carry on I have to stop typing again to wipe my tears and to stop retching. These memories can still make me feel sick to this day.)

Within a matter of seconds after the machine has been turned on an overwhelming feeling takes hold of my body that I cannot describe in words. The only way I can describe it is that it feels as though I am slowly dying. I feel incredibly sick, weak and very pale and it is as if life is draining out of my body. This is a feeling that you wouldn't even wish on your worst enemy. I am violently sick several times during this night. I struggle to move for the next three days. I start to become acquainted with the echo of small, helpless children crying out in pain and being sick at any given moment. I am now being monitored and tested vigilantly. The tests last for three days.

The only thing I can look forward to is when Dad, Andrew, Becki and Glen arrive. I cry very little through it all. However, seeing my family during visiting time and thinking about all that they do for me usually sets me off. I am not ashamed to tell you that my Mum stays with me during my treatment.

Mum is amazing. At night times she sleeps near to me on a little fold-out bed and we watch DVDs together to try to pass the time. She takes all my bottles of wee to be tested throughout the night, clears up my sick and says a prayer for me when I am feeling low.

The end of my first session is getting closer, but it still feels like a lifetime away. Once the final drip of mesna has gone into my body I am allowed to go home. Later this morning Dad arrives to take me home. I slowly walk toward the lift still feeling very fragile and weak. I open those big double doors again. For me it is time to leave Neverland or walk back through the wardrobe, but I consciously think that my time here is not over. It is far from over. It has only just begun.

Two hours later I arrive home and lie out on the sofa straight away. Lots of thoughts are running through my mind and I am now very conscious that my thinking and way of life is going to change. I want to reach for the phone to call a few mates, to see if they want to play football with me ... but it would be physically impossible. I'd like someone to call round for me and ask if I want to go swimming ... but now this Hickman line is in, I can't. At this point in time I am conscious of the fact that I won't be able to finish this journey by myself or even with the help of my friends and family. I remember the poem *Footprints*, which makes me very aware that I need God to carry me. Time passes slowly through to the evening where I lie awake in my bed. I listen to Tony Miller's healing CD and eventually fall to sleep. Unfortunately I wake up many times in the night due to nightmares. I awake suddenly believing that I have been asleep for hours, but it has only been five minutes. This is caused by the very strong anti-sickness drugs I have to take. The following morning I wake feeling very sick and incredibly weak. It feels like every time I even breathe it hurts or I think that I will be sick.

The following Wednesday I drive back to Leicester with Dad for my intravenous dose of Vincristine. My treatment protocol stated that this would happen on a weekly basis for the first month. Towards the end of the first week of treatment I start to feel very unwell. My temperature reaches 39 degrees and higher, so I am rushed to the local hospital where I have to spend the night. The round of golf I had earlier may have contributed to my condition. At the end of this week I sit down with my family to tell them that I physically can't do this again. I can't do one more session, let alone another six month's worth. I wanted the "overnight miracle" so that I wouldn't have to go through any more.

A week or so later I wake up to find big clumps of hair beside me on my pillow; my hair was beginning to fall out. I called my brother-in-law, Glen, to see if he would come round to shave my head as the bald patches were becoming too big to be covered. The head shaving ceremony quickly became a family affair as everyone gathered around to see the final strands of hair drop to the floor. In a matter of days all of my hair was totally gone, no eyebrows, no eyelashes. I was so bald you could nearly see what I was thinking!

I have many memories of Ward 27, but one of them is still very distinct to this day. I can remember lying asleep in the hospital bed and awakening to see people walking down the corridor carrying Christmas presents towards a little boy's room. As you will remember at the beginning of this chapter, I spoke of the same child who I met on my first visit to the ward. By this time he had become a little friend to me and I would often play my guitar to him. More and more people walked down the corridor holding presents, trying to bring a sense of joy in a very heavy atmosphere. His room was filled with Christmas decorations and in the corner of the room stood a large Christmas tree with bright lights and lots of colour. I asked one of the nurses what all the Christmas decorations and presents were for, since it was only the beginning of October. She replied in a sombre voice, "The family are doing Christmas early this year, Dave, as he's not going to be around for much longer." A few days later this small child left Neverland, walked back through the "wardrobe", never to return to this world, but I believe he went to be with Jesus where he is now free from any disease.

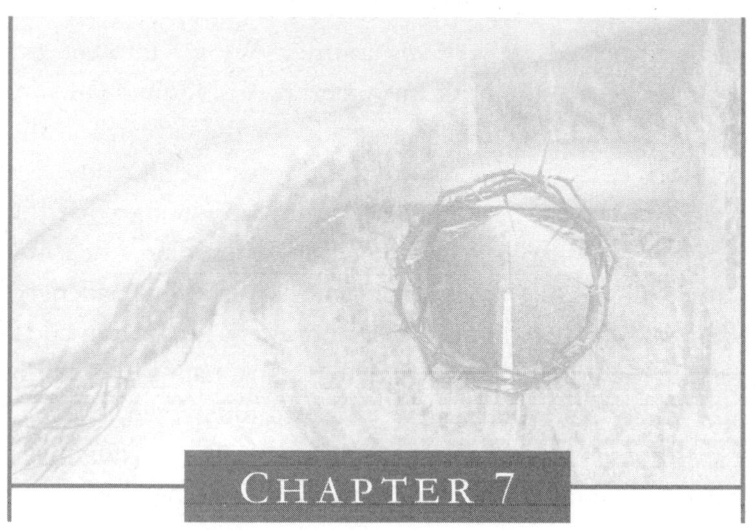

CHAPTER 7

RADIOTHERAPY

Dave

My treatment protocol stated that if the tumour responded well to the treatment, radiotherapy would not be needed. However, during my chemotherapy treatment new research identified that radiotherapy would be necessary in all circumstances. As you can imagine, having gone through all of the above to then to be confronted with the certainty of having intense radiotherapy, this news nearly made me give up. After having a long chat with my consultant where I shared my worries and concerns she underlined the fact that radiotherapy was going to be a necessity.

We eventually get the appointment to see a specialist consultant in Nottingham who will be taking me through this unexpected stage of my journey. We get into the car again and make the hour-long journey to Nottingham City Hospital. Dad has his money ready for the car park in the previous county, as he always does, so we are all ready! We walk into the waiting room and wait, wondering what the new consultant will be like. The door opens and I hear my name called. Out walks a man who is vertically challenged and looks like he was born in a laboratory. Dad, Mum and I go into the room and sit down. The consultant's first words are, "Who have you brought with you today then, David?" I am very tempted to inject a bit of humour by saying that I have brought my children with me, or something along those lines, but I resist and state that they are in fact my parents. This light atmosphere then leads to what is possibly the lowest point of my journey so far. After reading extensive lists of the effects of chemotherapy I am now presented with a new list of the effects of radiotherapy. Here they are:

- Cataracts
- Damage to pituitary gland
- Possible deformity to the bone structure on the right-hand side of my face
- Damage to the tear ducts
- Permanent loss of right eyebrow
- Permanent loss of right eyelashes
- Damage to the surface of the eye
- Damage to the skin surrounding the eye and the rear of my head

Now there's a list for you. Once this has been reported to us Dad goes rather white and leaves the room for a few minutes, whilst I request to lie down as I go pale and feel faint. The consultant now goes on to explain that the radiotherapy sessions are done daily and I could have up to twenty-five intense sessions that will take place alongside all of my remaining chemotherapy treatments. He also explains that I will have a mask made of my face that will be used to line up where the radiation is fired.

Afterwards, we get into the car and drive back to Lincoln. It is a very quiet journey home where I shed a few tears out of frustration at the situation. A few days later we make the trip back to Nottingham for the specialists to design and make my mask. I thought that this would be a simple procedure, but it turns out to be a very long and awful experience. I am asked to lie down on a surgical table whilst three white-coated technicians gather around me and get me into position. Two tubes are inserted into my nose and then hard setting rubber is poured all over my face. I am told to remain totally still for fifteen minutes until the rubber sets. Then plaster is poured on top of the rubber surface. I obviously can't see anything or even hear anything as the plaster has run over my eyes and ears, so I am in total darkness. I breathe through the two tubes in my nose without moving any part of my face. Eventually the mask begins to set and it takes two of the three staff to pull it away from my head. The mask fitting over, I am now ready for radiotherapy. In the meantime the consultant has been working on a radiotherapy plan where he calculates the correct dosage of radiation and works out the exit route for the radiation to leave my body.

Many in our nation remember 11th November for all the soldiers who died in the Second World War, but I also remember this day for two other reasons. Firstly, it was the day I started my radiotherapy and secondly it was the same day that I passed my driving test. One of our close family friends, Carol, offered to help with a lot of the driving to and from Nottingham for the next month. This worked well as Mum had never driven out of Lincoln before and Carol's help meant that I wouldn't have to permanently adopt the brace position when travelling to Nottingham.

So once again I get into a car and once again we drive to a hospital. An hour later we arrive and walk into the waiting room. The average age looks to be around 120 years, so I feel slightly out of place. My name is called and it is now time for me to start a whole new experience. I am constantly running the list of possibilities and side effects through my head as I follow the nurse down the corridor. I begin to pray a simple prayer that God will be with me in the treatment room and that He will take away all fear. I climb up onto a tall, long bed where I lie, subject to a large cylindrical machine facing down at me. My new mask is placed over my face and then bolted and clamped to the bed so that I can't move my head at all. The radiographers leave the room and talk to me over a speaker system from behind a thick lead wall.

The radiation is fired in two sections. I can't really describe how it feels but let's just say it is not pleasant. The radiotherapy doesn't affect me immediately the way that chemotherapy did, but it holds back its unpleasantness for a time to come.

As you will be aware, these last two chapters are quite long, possibly the longest in the book, but in truth I have only scratched the surface of what happened and the emotions I was feeling. One thing you do need to know is that every time I came out of hospital, no matter how I was feeling, church was still my number one priority. I never missed one worship or band practice throughout my entire course of treatment. Some people would say to me, "How can you still come to church when all of this is happening to you?" To me this seemed totally stupid, as church was the only place I wanted to be.

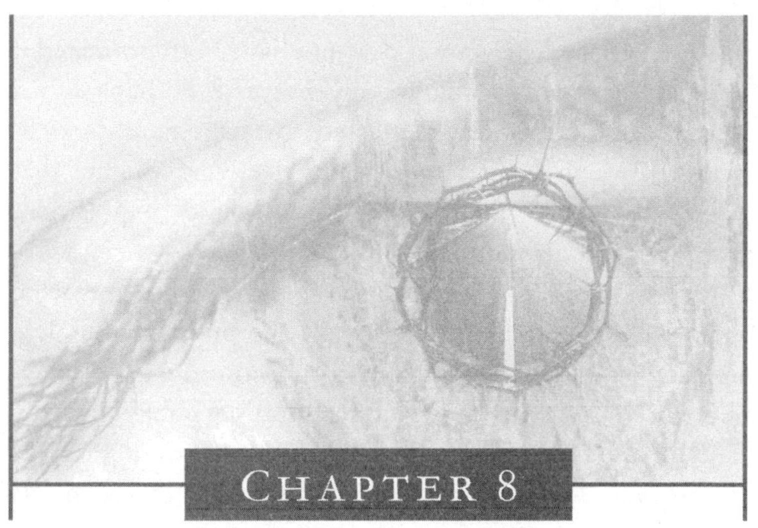

CHAPTER 8

MUD

Stuart

It is very difficult for parents when their own child becomes ill. It is also difficult for church leaders, who are used to standing with others, to have to stand with their own family members. A sixteen-year-old suddenly afflicted with disease throws up all kinds of questions. I have never been one for becoming angry towards God. I suppose I have walked with Him long enough to know that He can be trusted. However, I have often been more than ready to blame myself. So, as a father and a senior church leader, I am confronted with the question, "Why?" – a question asked by so many through the centuries. Was this something to do with me, some secret flaw in my faith-line or some prayerless door that had been left open? Surely my son would have been protected if I had been more vigilant in my prayers? Perhaps I had looked after others but neglected my own family's well-being? Though I tried to sideline fleeting thoughts that swept across my mind, was this some kind of judgment from God for just not being good enough?

One morning as I opened my Bible these thoughts were again seeking entrance. Was I really the problem? Surely a sixteen-year-old living in a Christian home could not amass enough black points to be under God's wrath? Then my random thoughts were stilled by the verse right there in front of me. The very question I had been battling with was in print before me in John chapter 9 – the story of how Jesus heals a man who was born blind. The question before me was, *"Rabbi, who sinned, this man or his parents that he was born blind?"* The answer Jesus gave became the bedrock for the dark journey ahead: *"Neither this man nor his parents sinned, but this happened so that the work of God might be displayed in his life."* Was God talking to me? Could it be that the end of the story would bring glory to God? It was clear this tumour had been permitted, but I knew that God's plans for my son were to do with victory and destiny. Jesus, as the light of the world, would become our light. As I heard these words faith began to rise and as I read on a strange excitement began to emerge somewhere deep within me.

Jesus did not lay hands on the man's eyes and command them to open. Instead He did an unacceptable thing (certainly to a British mind); He spat on the ground and made mud with the saliva. The thought of God spitting does challenge the religious, but any optician would have a problem with what followed. Jesus made a mud ball, slapped it on the man's eyes and said, "Go." The blind man now had a journey to make. He was to go to the pool of Siloam (meaning "sent") and wash the mud from his eyes before he would be able to see. These strange images began to find an interpretation within me. Perhaps there would be a journey to make before this was fully resolved and "mud" would be important in the process. In my diary I wrote, "Mud in the eye, I think, suggests treatment." Mud was a good description for what David would experience. I guess some would interpret this as a father clutching at straws, but I believe God was giving revelation for the journey ahead. Later, when sharing my thoughts with Derek Brown, a friend and church pastor in Aldershot, he reminded me of a conference five years earlier where we both shared in ministry. He had spoken about a challenge to apostolic ministry. His talk mentioned "Siloam" meaning "sent". It seemed that what God was doing through our church and network was being challenged. We were determined that this sending of ministries into communities, cities and nations was what we were called to. This vision was being challenged, but at the place of sending light would come.

Roger and Faith Forster, leaders of the Ichthus Fellowship, also shared with me that they sensed that church leaders in Britain were being targeted by the enemy and spoke over me, "You are like Peter. You're in prison, but you will be released." They also recounted the story of Jonah, who was confined but eventually released. I sensed my own call and journey was wrapped up in the destiny and release of my son. Perhaps some who are reading these words will find my interpretations a little tenuous. As you can imagine, we were aware of the many voices around us. I'm sure there were people who felt that conceding to any treatment was a lack of faith; others perhaps, thought we were ignoring the stark facts that were before us. However, the next part of the story underlined to us that we really were hearing from God.

Before the first session of chemotherapy we were going through agonies. David's eye was swollen with no outward sign that any healing had taken place. Were we weak in faith by pursuing what would be a very toxic regime that could severely affect his body? In the intangible world of the night hours I imagined waking to find the swollen eye had returned to normal, but looking into David's deformed eye I felt mocked and helpless. However, before we left to travel to the hospital in Leicester, Irene opened the UCB reading for the day. To our surprise and eventual wonder, the reading was about the healing of Naaman. "Naaman would have chosen any other river, but he had to be dipped in the muddy waters of the Jordan." It is certain we would not have chosen the river we were about to travel. We would have chosen the river of "overnight miracle", but another river was ahead.

Before his first session I talked to David about what would happen and declared, "David, you will have mud in the eye, you will be dipped in mud and on the seventh dip you will be healed." The chemotherapy protocol for David was nine treatments. We knew he must go through all nine, but declared he would be whole by the seventh "dip". I cannot prove it and what follows to conclude this chapter is an unusual sign. Though I had boldly affirmed these words there were low days when I wondered about the validity of the things we had heard. Could some of the experiences have been just coincidences? As the seventh session got closer I quietly prayed, "Lord, it would be really nice to have some confirmation about the seventh dip."

So there I stood nervously by David's bedside when he called out to me, "Dad, something strange is happening in my chest." He went on to tell me that the Hickman line that had been surgically fitted in his chest was coming out! "Don't be silly," I lovingly said. "You've played golf, you've done all kinds of activities for weeks, it's surgically fitted and it's not going to move." But within seconds the line began to slowly slip from his chest. David went white and I inwardly panicked imagining blood gushing from the hole in his chest. We called for help. David's designated nurse came and thrust a wad of bandages into the hole. She looked as though this happened regularly, but called for emergency help as things didn't look good. Following being checked out his nurse said warmly, "David, this is OK, we can administer the remaining treatment through a cannula in the back of your hand. So, it's good news, you won't have to have the Hickman line removed surgically!"

Whatever the implications were for the medical profession, for us this was a confirmation of a miracle!

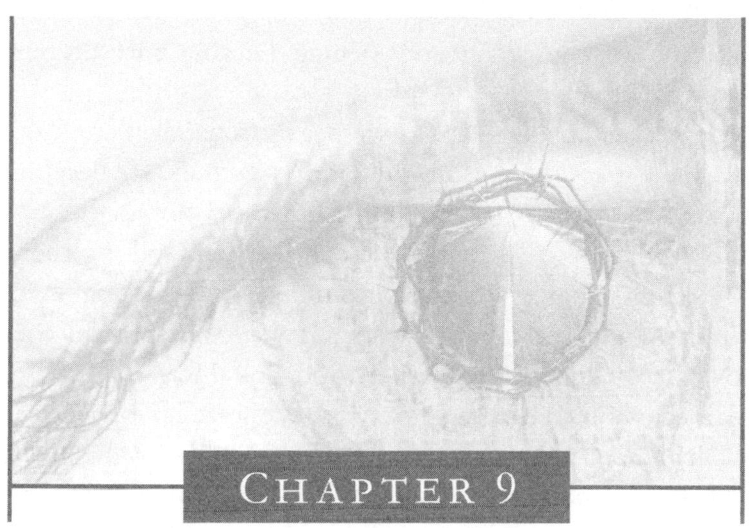

Chapter 9

Prayer Strategy

Stuart

When the problems of this world bring you to your knees you're in the perfect position to pray. We knew that everything was going to hinge on prayer and that we would have to enter unfamiliar faith territory. In fact, we felt like Jesus' disciples who said, "Lord teach us how to pray." We were aware that this was not to do with the number of hours we spent in prayer, but would be to do with dependency on the Holy Spirit. We felt totally inadequate, which opened a door for the Spirit to help us in our weakness. We were at the base of a huge learning curve not knowing exactly how high the mountain ahead would be. We also came to the conclusion that words are not enough as we began to discover that groaning and sighing became part of our intercession.

However, step-by-step, as we began to handle Scripture, we knew that Jesus was on the journey with us. He became to us *"the great high priest who sympathizes with our weaknesses."* We also began to discover the father heart of God together. We rehearsed over and over His unique and personal love for each of us and as I look back today we were proving the love of a triune God, Father, Son and Holy Spirit. We learned so much by simply praying. We were no longer just talking about prayer, we were doing it. The following are a few things that we began to learn. It is our prayer that someone reading this now will be encouraged and helped, which is our main reason for documenting our journey.

Praying through Scripture

We gathered a list of helpful verses that we believe the Holy Spirit highlighted to us and proclaimed them every day. We also wrote them down so that the prayer team could stand in agreement with us. All of the following were among the passages we regularly quoted:

> *"He said, 'If you listen carefully to the voice of the LORD your God and do what is right in his eyes, if you pay attention to his commands and keep all his decrees, I will not bring on you any of the diseases I brought on the Egyptians, for I am the LORD, who heals you.' "*
>
> (Exodus 15:26)

> *"He said: 'Listen, King Jehoshaphat and all who live in Judah and Jerusalem! This is what the LORD says to you: "Do not be*

afraid or discouraged because of this vast army. For the battle is not yours, but God's." ' "

(2 CHRONICLES 20:15)

" 'Neither this man nor his parents sinned,' said Jesus, 'but this happened so that the work of God might be displayed in his life.' "

(JOHN 9:3)

"This is the confidence we have in approaching God: that if we ask anything according to his will, he hears us. And if we know that he hears us – whatever we ask – we know that we have what we asked of him."

(1 JOHN 5:14–15)

"Finally, be strong in the Lord and in his mighty power."

(EPHESIANS 6:10)

"Because of the LORD's great love we are not consumed,
for his compassions never fail.
They are new every morning;
great is your faithfulness."

(LAMENTATIONS 3:22–23)

"But he was pierced for our transgressions,
he was crushed for our iniquities;
the punishment that brought us peace was upon him,
and by his wounds we are healed."

(ISAIAH 53:5)

Standing in Unity

We made sure that we stood together in absolute unity. The roots of cancer are rebellious cells that have grown independently from the body. It was important that we spoke with one voice. Often we would literally pray the words in unison and also make sure we were never passive when others were praying so that "amen" was not just the formal end to a prayer, but a positive statement of agreement.

Different Types of Praying

Together we learned the importance of soaking prayer. This was where we would listen to a worship CD and simply relax and receive from God. During these times tiredness would leave us and faith would come. We often would gently pray over David for healing and for a revelation of the Father's love.

Then there was battling prayer where we filled the air with loud intercession. On these occasions deliverance was our focus. This involved speaking to the cancer. This was to us like moving a mountain. We learned how powerful our words could be and also speaking in languages of the Spirit brought higher levels of engagement. One Sunday evening I looked David in the eyes and commanded the cancer to move in the name of Jesus. Our simple belief is that Jesus has given His followers permission to use His name.

We also discovered the importance of bedtime prayers. As we all know the dark hours of night can be our time of greatest vulnerability. This is when the imagination can go into overdrive. We were also aware that sleep was very important. This was when we were introduced to a CD from our good friend Tony Miller who reads healing verses interspersed with gentle music. The combination of his rich deep voice and scriptural truth opened the doorway for a good night's sleep.

Speaking in tongues released great blessing, particularly when we were under unusual pressure. Due to the unrelenting daily radiotherapy David's eye began to suffer. As we entered 2005 his eye became very painful, until one day when he woke the pain was so bad that we were advised to drive to Leicester for yet another meeting with the eye consultant. I could tell that David was frustrated, so as we got into the car I began to speak in tongues. As we reached the main road I stopped speaking and set my attention on the drive ahead. "What are you doing?" David asked. "I thought you said you were going to speak in tongues, was that it?" He then suggested that I should speak all the way to Leicester because he felt better when I prayed. So that's what I did and the further we drove the more faith-filled we became. The specialist said David had conjunctivitis due to the treatment, prescribed some eye-drops and another crisis was dealt with. This was another example of the medical and spiritual working hand in hand.

Set Prayers

I have to confess that I have never been a great fan of liturgical praying. I have tended to favour spontaneous praying from the heart. However, these prayers have sometimes lacked substance. So alongside our usual kind of prayers we developed some that we could use on a daily basis. I have included one or two model prayers throughout this book. We issued the following prayer to all our family members so that we could pray in unity every day.

> "As a family we pray for David. We stand together in unity to pray for his total healing. We believe that Jesus came into the world to destroy the works of the evil one. We therefore pray that the lump behind David's eye be uprooted and cast out. Use the medical profession for Your glory and see to it that David is made totally whole so that he can become the person he is destined to be. May Jesus be glorified and may the love and peace of God overshadow our lives. Amen."

Next is a copy of a prayer that remained at the side of David's bed for the duration of the radiotherapy treatment.

This is my radiotherapy prayer:

> "Father God, we bring David before You today. We declare that Jesus Christ, the Son of God, came into the world to destroy the work of the devil. We trust in the finished work of the cross of Jesus Christ and believe that by His stripes we were healed. In Your mercy, Lord, we ask that You be a shield to David. We pray that You will protect his eyebrow, pituitary gland and tear ducts from all harm. May this radiotherapy be like the arrow of the Lord that harms all rogue cells and misses the good ones. We declare that all things are possible with God and confess Daniel 3:27: *'They saw that the fire had not harmed their bodies, nor was there a hair of their heads singed; their robes were not scorched, and there was no smell of fire on them.'* We also declare the truth of

Exodus 14:13: *'Do not be afraid. Stand firm and you will see the deliverance the LORD will bring you today. The Egyptians you see today you will never see again.'* Lord of Compassion, hear our prayer. Amen."

Bite-sized Prayers

Often we would begin a prayer meeting with the question, "What can we believe God for tonight?" We would then share what we felt God was challenging us to pray for and go for it. Sometimes we would face one another with one person praying and the other agreeing. In this way we faced situations one prayer at a time. We soon discovered that we were walking a daily miracle path together.

Laying On of Hands

On many occasions we put David in the centre of a prayer circle and people would lay hands on his head. We also, on a regular basis, called the elders of the church to lay their hands on him and anoint him with oil in obedience to the Scriptures.

Thanksgiving and Praise

After each prayer session we made it our policy to remember to say, "Thank You." It would have been so easy to keep bringing our requests, but we felt that it was important that after every answer to prayer we made space for thanks and praise. We were very conscious of the fact that often in the Bible people failed to return to give thanks to Jesus. We learned to offer praise as our prayers were answered.

Remembering Others

I have become very aware that many people in our world have no one praying for them. I am also conscious that many people's stories don't have a happy ending. Our prayer times began increasingly to include others and became a model within our church. May what we have learned be a help and encouragement to others.

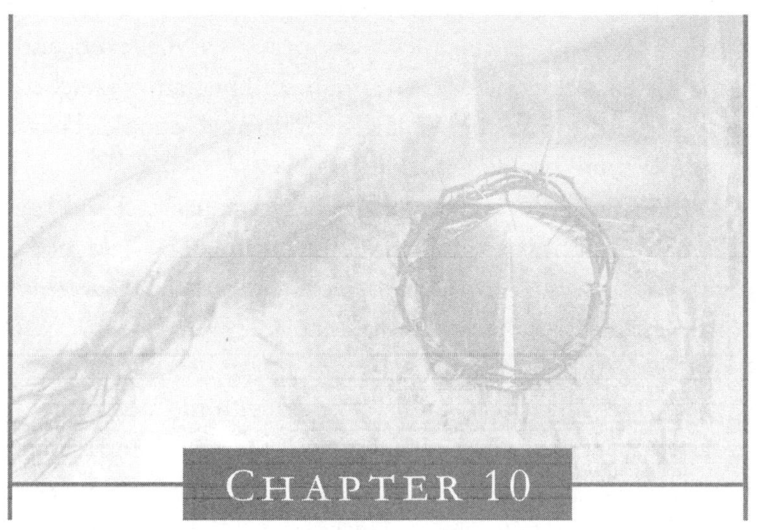

CHAPTER 10

WHEN GOD SPEAKS

Stuart

I would hate to live in a silent world where the voice of God is not heard. We thank God for the Bible which brings light to every step we take. I'm also thankful for the gift of prophecy and use this chapter to illustrate the fact that through our months of trial God was constantly speaking. Some of these words were affirming words where the ancient words of Scripture seemed perfectly crafted for our unique needs. Some of the words were words of revelation giving us insights into things we could never have naturally known. Other words were words of defence and safety. Some words were general principles that apply to all believers and some were specific to our own situation. The names attached to these words prove that God speaks through people. These people faithfully delivered hope to us.

During the initial stages of David's treatment I did my best to be faithful to ministry commitments. I had been invited to speak at Terry Virgo's highly influential leadership conference at Brighton Conference Centre. I heard that Rambabu, a healing evangelist from India, was also a guest speaker. I took one of David's T-shirts with me, determined to have it prayed over. I delivered the shirt and asked Rambabu to pray over it. His dark eyes looked firmly into mine with a piercing look of compassion as he declared, "Your son will be OK."

Mark Hutton, one of our pastors, had a dream where he saw two dogs were attacking us. In the dream the dogs were killed. Later, Rachel Hickson brought us two sets of pictures. She said that God had shown her that David had cancer (she checked the information was correct with a pastor who knew of our circumstances) and that the enemy had a five-year strategy against my ministry. She then shared two pictures. The first was of fields in Texas where cattle were free to roam. She then saw the cattle being confined stage by stage until they were all confined into a small area. She then saw two dogs were sent to bring harm. (Sometime earlier I had a dream where two robbers were robbing a house.) In the second picture Rachel saw Russian dolls which became smaller and smaller and told me that the enemy wanted to confine us, but went on to say that God had confined the season of the attack and had confined the enemy's work. We were, in fact, told by our consultant that the tumour was "confined" behind David's eye. We realized that this was big stuff, but God was speaking. Though the enemy had plans, God's plans and purposes were bigger.

At Grapevine, our Ground Level annual celebration, Heidi Baker, who is seeing great miracles happening in Mozambique, sat cross-legged with David, prayed and spoke words of encouragement over him. Then, of course, our own friends continued to contribute. Philip Hickerton from New Life said, "You will look back on these days and say they were good because God will erase anxieties and fears. You will remember God's grace, love and kindness." Kathy Paton added, "The enemy is like a wolf with no teeth – just noise." Slim quoted Psalm 144:1, the verse that released David's plectrum finger. Grace declared, "You will have double for your trouble", which we will return to later. She also quoted Isaiah 10:27, stating the yoke was broken through the anointing. Another verse she gave we have prayed many times: *"We have escaped like a bird out of the fowler's snare; the snare has been broken, and we have escaped"* (Psalm 124:7). Faith Forster phoned one day with exactly the same verse. Then there was Ron and Barbara Tempest who became like spiritual parents to us. Ron was involved with Bryn Jones for many years before he died. They prophesied over David with regard to his future life and ministry, saying, "What is happening in him is more important than what is happening to him." They spoke of a future ministry of healing and even miracles. This has now been endorsed by many including Duane White and Denny Cramer from America.

I am taking time to record these details to show how many people stood with us and also to illustrate the intensity of the battle. On Tuesday 4th November, 2003, I left for a meeting at Waverley Abbey House. I was to attend a Round

Table hosted by my good friend, Gerald Coates. I have connected with Gerald for many years and have always valued these meetings. Over these two days a number of people spoke over our situation. I greatly valued the wise words of Steve Chalke who seemed to understand our plight in a special way. Peter Lyne declared that, "No weapon forged against us would prosper" and Derek Brown read James 1:12–13.

In one session something happened in the realm where words are not enough. We were sitting in a circle sharing issues for prayer. When it came to my turn I didn't know where to begin. David Carr, seeing my dilemma, stood to his feet and slowly walked towards me with his arms outstretched. If you've seen David you'll know this was quite an inspiring sight. I was sensing a bear hug was on the way and if you've seen me, let's just say I'm not the biggest of people. From the other side of the room he said, "This is what God feels," and kept walking towards me. When he reached me he unexpectedly convulsed into tears and then came the hug and a kiss on the top of my head. I think David was as surprised as I was. You can imagine the drama. All I know is that I became aware that the Father was weeping with us just like Jesus wept in the house of Martha and Mary. Gerald sensing the prophetic moment poured profuse amounts of water over my head praying for God's cleansing and healing. The water mingled with my tears. It reminded me of a prophecy he had given me years before that I would cry in private, I would cry in public and I would cry in front of large crowds. I gladly affirm the accuracy of these words.

While I'm being a little vulnerable let me just mention one more crying episode. I was in a Grace Network conference in the USA when Jack Groblewski and Francois van

Niekerk took me to one side. We have learned to be honest and open to a deep level together. As I confessed to them areas of disappointment and even a sense of being damaged I shared my pains and let it all out. The dam broke and I wept like a child. This was a healing moment and as I'm sitting writing this today, as Irene reads the newspaper the other side of the coffee table, we are aware the tears are still near the surface. Perhaps these feelings will make us better parents and leaders in the church. For some the experiences we have shared would make them bitter, for us we pray they will make us better.

I close this chapter with one more leadership gathering. This time the venue was Mulberry House at a meeting hosted by Terry Virgo. Dave's treatment was all completed, the final scan had been taken. It was Friday morning and I was waiting for a phone call. It was difficult for me to concentrate on the first session of the day. The minutes ticked by as I examined the old wooden beams in the room. At 11.20am my mobile phone rang. It was Irene. Through sobs and with a wavering but joyful voice she said, "There is no evidence of any disease."

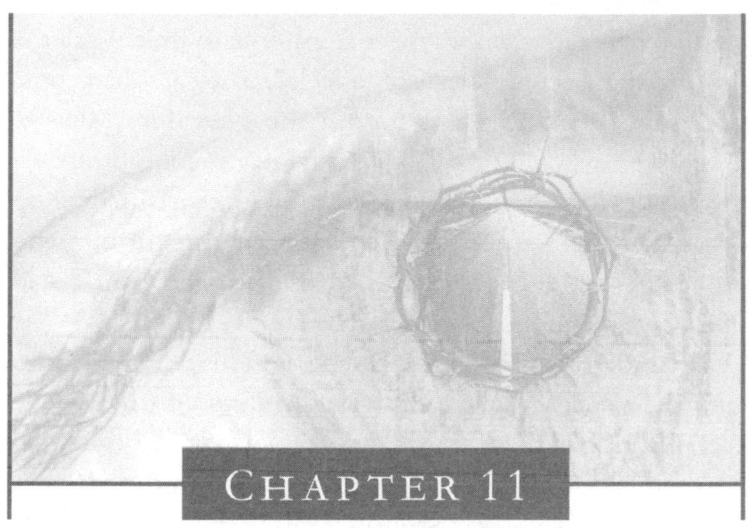

ANGELS

Stuart

I believe in angels. There are, of course, the real angels who are God's powerful messengers of fire. Then there are human angels who with angel-like compassion serve God's people. The Bible also tells us that we can entertain angels without knowing it, so sometimes heaven and earth are separated by a very thin veil.

We were helped with lifts in cars, food on our table and support and affirmation on all sides. I know that as I write this chapter we cannot name everyone who helped us. I am also aware that most would rather remain anonymous as that's the kind of people they are. Those who don't get a mention are known by God and also by us as we catch the glint in their eye when we meet from time to time. I call the first group of people "ministry angels". They are the people who served us and cared for us; the New Life Ministry Team who wholeheartedly released me to concentrate on my family; the Ground Level Team who kept "holding up our arms". I remember Paul Randerson, from Norfolk, who drove over to Leicester to pray for David. The team would often encircle me for focused prayer.

Then there was the angel, Duane, and his wife Kris, who with their children decided to stay in Lincoln for a whole year. Duane had prophesied that David would be healed and it would have been very easy for him to return to the States and keep in touch by telephone. However, he didn't just speak prophetic words he walked them out alongside us.

Jeff and Kay Lucas, for us, also came into the angel category. The angel Derek, is familiar to many, but for the purpose of this book has to stand aside for the angel Jeff, who always seemed to arrive at the most crucial of times. One evening he placed a bottle of champagne in our home ready for the celebration that would take place many weeks ahead, a very brave angelic gesture.

The second group I want to mention are known to us as "medical angels". They appeared in blue overalls and nurse's uniforms. The team on Ward 27 were wonderful to us. Surrounded by extreme suffering they remained professional, positive and caring. When they were around us we felt safe. Surgeons, consultants and eye specialists all played their part. David struck up quite a relationship with many. One event I remember with fondness was hearing David shouting, "Women drivers, no survivors!" as a nurse was pushing him in a wheelchair back from surgery. The anaesthetic contributed to a new boldness!

Angel Carol, from New Life, stood quietly by Irene's side on numerous occasions, driving her and David to Nottingham for his radiotherapy treatment on a regular basis.

I now move on to stories that are a little more difficult to comment on. According to the Bible, angels are sent to minister to God's people. Psalm 91:11 says,

"For he will command his angels concerning you
to guard you in all your ways;
they will lift you up in their hands,
so that you will not strike your foot against a stone."

I don't think it's going too far to suggest that if angels are concerned when someone hurts their foot, then they are equally concerned for people who are facing major health issues. From time to time our family were certainly aware that unusual levels of help and love were reaching our world, particularly in prayer sessions when waves of wellbeing rippled around us.

We were also aware that David was given unusual strength. So much so that I am convinced that many members in our church never really knew the extent of the challenge. David never missed a church meeting, simply because he never wanted to. Strength was coming from somewhere. He continued, throughout his treatment, to enjoy life to the full. Within hours of a gruelling two days in hospital he would be out on the golf course playing eighteen holes. I don't remember any hint of him giving up or backing off. I choose to believe that angels were allocated to his cause to strengthen him.

Now on to the more unusual story. Following months of chemotherapy we now had to face twenty-five consecutive days of radiotherapy. David found the making of his protective mask one of the hardest things to endure. He has already shared this experience in his radiotherapy chapter. What David didn't mention was that the plaster-of-Paris replica of his head was usefully employed to frighten Irene. Seeing him walk into the room with his "head" under his right arm was a bit scary.

We were unsure what to expect as we entered Nottingham City Hospital. Though the administration of the radiotherapy would not be painful, we were all concerned about the consequences. During the short treatment session David saw a blue flash of light. Nervous that his retina might have been harmed and not knowing exactly what took place during treatment, we asked the radiographer about the flashing blue light. She said that she had never heard of it happening before and assured us there would not be a problem.

On day two, however, the same thing happened again so we asked to speak to the consultant. He told us in no uncertain terms that he had treated the eyes of hundreds of people and had never heard of the "flashing light" and suggested that David must have imagined it. But during each successive treatment David experienced the same flashing light and knew exactly when it would happen. On one occasion the radiographer saw David touching his mask and reaching out as if to catch hold of an imaginary arm. When asked, "What are you doing?" he explained that he sensed someone was close and actually touching his mask. As we discussed what may have been going on we chose to believe that angels were present. During following sessions, not only was there the blue flash of light but he also felt someone "tapping" around his eye. Again, because in the

Western world we don't handle "mystery" too well, we were reticent to say much more.

During one of our regular telephone updates to Jack Groblewski in the USA, I recounted the details to him and his immediate reply was, "That's really interesting. I have just heard of a well-known prophet who flew into Scotland declaring that God was going to move in a fresh way in the realm of healing in the UK." Jack went on to say that this prophet then made the comment, "Blue is the colour of healing." This American prophet was suggesting that a sign of the new wave of healing was "blue light".

Recently, Jonathan Conrathe, a respected healing evangelist who has ministered all over the world, told me that in his own ministry when people receive healing they often mention seeing blue flashes of light. He said that some claim to have seen angels bathed in blue light.

When Peter was being miraculously released from prison in Acts 12:9 the Bible says, *"Peter followed him out of the prison, but he had no idea that what the angel was doing was really happening."* So, if Peter wasn't sure what was going on, perhaps you could be gracious with us? All I know is that angels exist and they exist to serve God's people. I believe that men and angels have accompanied us on our journey.

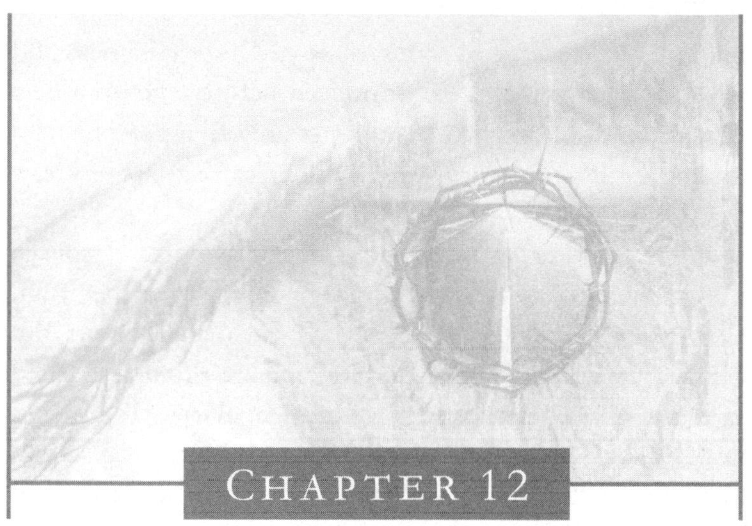

CHAPTER 12

OWLS, RAINBOWS AND THUNDERCLAPS

Stuart

As I have got older I have become increasingly aware that more is going on than we first realize. Often we have a limited understanding of how God speaks to us. In fact, God speaks in many and varied ways if we have ears to hear and eyes to see. In the Bible spiritual truths are often linked with physical things that can be touched or seen. Jesus often communicated spiritual truths through illustrations taken from the physical world. Often it is during the pressures and battles of life that we become aware of God's greatness and wisdom. Things that were unnoticed before take on a new dimension of meaning. These things are often personal and unique. I think of them as God's calling cards to let us know that He is still with us.

For a number of years now owls have had a special meaning for us as a family. Before going any further I am aware that some would associate owls with occult activity, but actually owls were created by God and are often associated with wisdom. The following is not essential to our story, but gives a glimpse of how God used certain situations to give an awareness of His presence. I have often seen white owls at important times in my life. I vividly remember a trip when Irene and I were wondering whether she was pregnant with David. As we were discussing the possibility, a white owl flew slowly in front of our car. On his first day at school, above David's coat peg, was a picture of an owl. On his first trip to England our friend, Jack Groblewski, stayed in an old house in the leafy village of Hambledon. When he opened his bedroom window the following morning, an owl was sitting on the windowsill. From that day on we exchanged owl stories and on one or two occasions when special things were going to happen, we would both see a white owl. I have asked David to share the following story which took place after his final chemotherapy session:

> "I was driving home late one night and that evening I was feeling fairly low. I started to think about the next few months and all of the challenges that lay ahead. I started to pray and ask God for a sign that He was with me and that He would guide me through all of the trials. Within seconds, a large brown owl started flying

alongside the car. This was amazing, but God really went out of His way for me with what happened next. I started to thank God for the sign, but I really wanted to see more, like everyone does I suppose. With that, the owl got closer and closer to the car until the tip of its wing was nearly touching. Just before I turned off the road, the owl swooped round in front of the car. Its wing brushed the windscreen and its face looked directly at me, literally just centimetres away. This was an experience that I will never forget. God always shows up when we need Him, without fail."

And now from owls to rainbows. Is it really possible that God would arrange a rainbow display to give our small family a sense of security? I believe it is. The rainbow signifies the promises of a covenant-keeping God over His creation. Through the centuries countless people must have looked to the skies and recognised that God's promises are bigger than the storms we face. It's also amazing to me that this wonderful sign has often been hijacked for other purposes, but the bottom line is it remains a reminder of God's promises in a fallen world.

Becki and Glen were driving to Leicester not knowing what to expect. Irene had just phoned and sounded quite distressed. They would soon hear the results of the biopsy. Becki was feeling quite low when suddenly a strong thought came into her mind. She seemed to hear the words, "Look out of the window, look up!" She looked out of the left-hand side window and high in the sky was a large rainbow. There was no evidence of rain, but there it was high above the car. Becki then had the strong impression, "God always keeps His promises; He is always faithful."

I greeted Glen and Becki in the corridor outside David's room and delivered the news that David had cancer. After sharing tears together we all went into the ward trying to make sense of what was taking place. Later in the evening we accompanied the family to the lift. Before leaving, Becki shared with Irene the story of the rainbow and said, "God will keep His promises."

On 19th June, 2003, Pete Atkins entered the following in his prayer journal. I have recounted these personal prayer requests with his permission as a source of encouragement:

19.06.03 00.10

"Due for David's biopsy result later today. Yesterday, I felt you asked us to pray against the gathering storm. In the morning I was mindful of Roger's and another's picture of gathering clouds over the Bell family. I felt you wanted us to pray to break the storm and stand against the storm breaking over them. Then at 18.30 as they left their house for the prayer meeting there was a most incredible thunderclap, which didn't affect them as they had just got into the car and shut the door. However, lightning hit Tony and Tracy's house and left the TV, PS1 and PS2 and computer dead and smoking; the health centre car park surface was hit and Julia and David's house. Again this evening (4th or 5th time) 30 gathered to pray as we began – or by the end. 30 'mighty men'.

There have been signs of Your intervention all through from the timing of scans to thunderstorms. I believe we have prayed all we can or should have locally with wonderful backing nationally (UK leaders: Roger and Faith Forster, Gerald, Tony and Hannah, Ian Andrews, Jeff Lucas and overseas in Texas, Zambia,

Reinhard Bonnke's association, Pretoria, Mal Fletcher etc.). Grant us grace tomorrow, Father. Grant us Your wisdom, grant us all peace and encouragement. We all agreed tonight for:

1. Complete healing
2. Encouraging words tomorrow
3. Strength and grace for the journey."

Our three requests were granted.

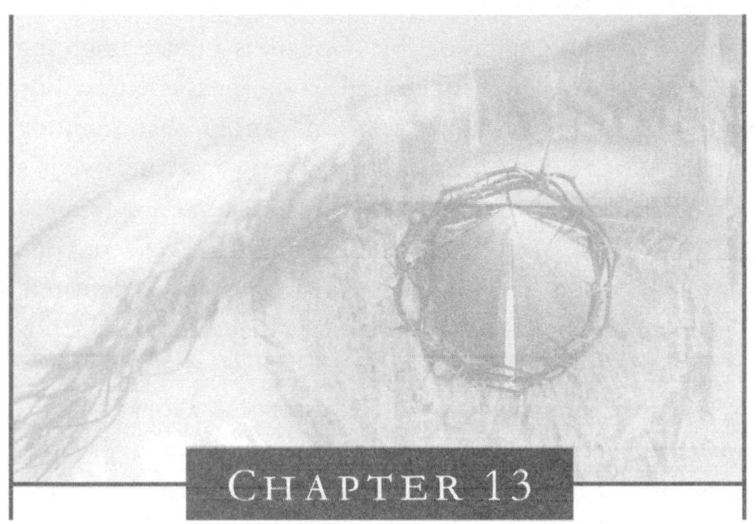

FACING GIANTS

Stuart

I have tried to write as a dad rather than as a pastor. However, I have included this chapter as it illustrates that preaching and teaching are meant to equip us for living. It is important that what we say from platforms is lived out in our daily lives. It is a strange feeling to be challenged by one's own teaching. The words of Jesus come to mind, *"Physician, heal yourself!"* (Luke 4:23). David had to face his giant. Giants represent that which is bigger than us. They represent something that, in the natural, we are incapable of defeating, a person or thing of great size. In the biblical account of 1 Samuel chapter 17, Goliath is described in great detail. The words used paint a picture of the size of the battle. The odds are impossible. Goliath is a trained fighting machine and David is portrayed as an inexperienced boy who was more suited to watching sheep than fighting battles. When we are facing giants getting a perspective is a very difficult thing. In the Bible story Goliath is not going to go away. The Israeli army is not going to wake up one morning to find him gone. The giant had to be defeated. There are certain things about Goliath that apply to all kinds of giants that we may have to face.

The first thing the story tells us is that Goliath had a *reputation*. He was the champion of the Philistines. He was the strongest and the biggest among his people and the sight of him brought great fear into the camp. As our David faced the "Big C", the very word itself carried with it a fear factor even before the details were known.

Around Goliath was also *magnification*. Everything about this champion was larger than life. He was over nine feet tall and had heavy armour weighing five thousand shekels. He had a bronze javelin swung across his shoulders, Rambo fashion, and a spear that was like a weaver's rod. He stood and loudly shouted curses across the battle lines defying God and His people. No wonder it says that, *"Saul and all the Israelites were dismayed and terrified."*

We learned during our journey that thoughts and imaginations become fertile soil for all kinds of fears to germinate. We will share later the importance of capturing these fears to make them subject to a higher power, the power of the Word of God.

Next there was *intimidation*. The ranting giant mercilessly shouted abuse and challenged anyone to fight him. He was secure in his badness. In real terms Goliath was suggesting that if the God of Israel really was alive, then surely someone would have the guts to stand up for their beliefs. Even King Saul, who was bigger than most men, wasn't looking for a fight and kept his head down every time the gauntlet was laid down.

For me, powerlessness was my biggest challenge. I've preached on giants, healing, overcoming, breakthrough, faith, prayer, deliverance and a multitude of other subjects from both the Old and New Testaments for the best part of thirty years, but now a giant was sounding pretty convincing.

Finally there was *repetition*. The defiance was not a single episode. Like a dripping tap this was a day-after-day issue. The more Goliath spoke the more powerful he became. His booming voice threw out the daily challenge, "Somebody stop me!"

There were days when we woke up hoping that everything had gone away. We tried to picture our lives with the problem sorted. However, the giant had to be faced!

As the Bible story continues the scene changes its emphasis towards David. There couldn't be more of a contrast. David is described as the youngest of Jesse's sons. You may well remember that he was the one who was ignored when the prophet Samuel visited the house earlier. His three older brothers were on the front line and David was only present because he had carried supplies of bread and cheese from his father. The Bible goes out of its way to describe how unqualified he was to face Goliath. In fact, his brothers disown him when he begins to suggest that someone ought to sort out the uncircumcised Philistine. However, David proves to be more than expected. In the fields of Bethlehem he had learned the art of hitting bottles with a slingshot. More than that, he had on occasions faced lions and bears in order to protect his father's flock. I have come to the conclusion that when things come against us there is often more in us than we realize, but the secret to David's success had deeper roots.

David knew God and knew that God had a purpose for his life. Everyone had weighed up the battle in the natural, but David knew that the battle belonged to the Lord. When he offered his services to Saul, Saul offered his own armour, but David felt more equipped with his shepherd's gear than the normal weapons of warfare. To cut a long story short, David faced his giant. The fact was, Goliath was bigger and stronger than David, but the truth was the stone from the sling went round and round and the giant came tumbling down. The bigger they are the harder they fall!

Our David also became a giant slayer, but the battle belonged to the Lord.

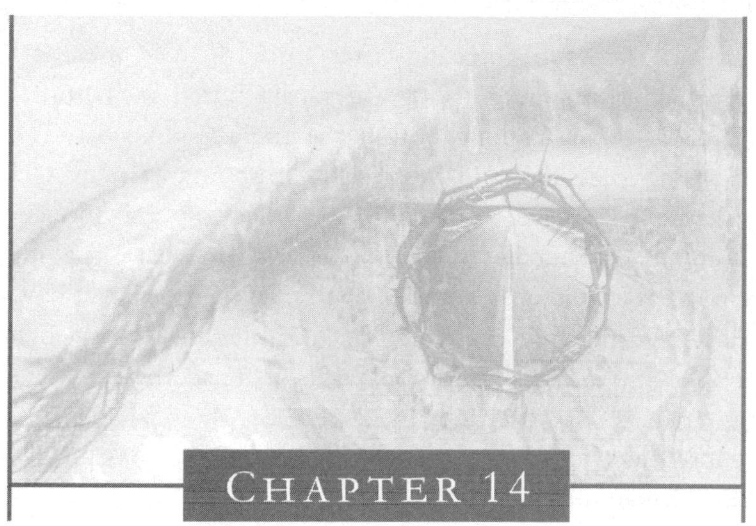

CHAPTER 14

FROM CARPET TO CONFLICT

Stuart

Let me return for a while to what I described earlier as our "golden years". In 1994 there was an air of expectancy around many churches in the UK. I remember reading headlines like, "'It wasn't my fault,' says vicar". The story went on to describe how a vicar had "blessed" his congregation at the end of the service and, as he did so, a strange phenomenon broke out among the people. Some burst into laughter, others fell to the floor; an unexpected sight in your average Anglican Church. Similar stories began to spread. Holy Trinity Church in Brompton, London, reported unusual levels of blessing after one of their members returned from the Airport Vineyard Church in Toronto, Canada. It wasn't long before the media spoke of "The Toronto Blessing". On hearing of "rumours of revival" I telephoned Gerald Coates, the leader of the Pioneer Network of Churches in London, to ask him what was going on. He told me further stories of strange happenings. I have described my first encounter of "the blessing" in my first book, *In Search of Revival*, and have no space here to give any details. However, our lives were deeply impacted. Our church met together night after night as a new passion for God began to refresh us.

I was invited to speak in many places that were new to me, and was excited to see people's lives changed and blessed. On numerous occasions I was invited to speak in Toronto and saw firsthand things that I had previously read of in historic accounts of revival. There was an air of expectancy and many believed the Church in the UK was going to experience a major revival similar to the Welsh revivals at the beginning of the twentieth century. For readers who have no experience of those days it is worth mentioning that in church services people would often fall to the floor as the power of God touched their lives. This led to what some described as "carpet time". People would lie on the floor enjoying God's presence. Some would laugh, others would cry. We began to realize that some never "felt" anything at all, but we encouraged them to remain open to what God was doing. Church programmes were disrupted, but we were convinced that we needed to yield to what the Holy Spirit was doing.

In our own context there was a regular flow of stories of how God was changing people's lives. Irene and I certainly appreciated God's refreshing power in our lives. From being a small boy I had looked to the day when I would experience "revival" and we were certainly being given a taster. During a visit to Pittsburgh, USA, I became aware that this wave of blessing had the potential to change cities. For a season we saw people reconciled, churches changed, and a new desire for Christians to unite together. A fresh wave of prayer was rising in our land and across the world.

I remember one warm day in London attending a meeting arranged by Gerald Coates. We were due to meet the Queen of Romania who would share her newfound faith. In the morning a number of us met for prayer and sharing. As we prayed together our ordered prayer became severely disrupted. Many were engulfed with laughter, others showed signs of being thoroughly "drunk". Of course, they were not *"drunk as you suppose"* as it was still early morning. Doors into the room were blocked with bodies as down the drive the royal car made its way to our venue. Gerald didn't appear flustered by this, he just climbed through the front window and ushered our guest into another room. It was difficult to bring things to order but, before long, we were listening to the Queen of Romania as though nothing had happened. Looking back these were holy moments. Revival was in the air.

Reports were not limited to our Isles either. I was invited to Osaka, Japan, and witnessed the "refreshing" Eastern style. For the Japanese, to lie on the floor was culturally unusual; shoes are removed before entering a room but, lie on floors they did! In fact, I was intrigued to see that, as people fell, they were placed in neat rows and wrapped in blankets. Large piles of cushions were also around the edge of the room, ready to be placed under people's heads.

I remember thinking, "Church is getting interesting!" As you would expect many people questioned, "Is this really God?". Others dubbed it emotionalism. Some even suggested that we had all been led into deception, but others wisely linked what was happening to the Scriptures and began to benefit. I also tried to bring a context by reading accounts of past revivals which, at the time, were equally controversial. I'm sure some jumped on the bandwagon, and I am also conscious that some were touched but not changed. This led to a number of leaders genuinely asking if the benefits of what was taking place would be long-lasting. It is true to say that what happened fell short of the high levels of expectation.

Pensacola, USA, also became a focal point for a new evangelistic fervour, and huge crowds made a pilgrimage there for a renewing of their faith. I am convinced that these were a genuine move of God's Spirit and where leadership brought guidance and balance, many churches were strengthened. All moves of God are challenged and it would be true to say that a number of leaders became disillusioned, even cynical.

One evening, Irene and I were discussing the things that had taken place in our lives. As we talked freely about God's goodness, we also discussed the meaning of the "refreshing" God had brought to us. We continue to long for historic revival, but we came to the conclusion that God always has a purpose with the things He does. We reasoned that maybe the refreshing was designed not just to make us feel good, but to strengthen us on the inside. Perhaps, like Joseph, the years of abundance may provide food for the barren years ahead. Our reflections brought us to the conclusion that we needed to receive everything God was pouring over our

my story

Dave Bell

the diagnosis

EXAM

Ward: R37 Date: 11/06/2003 @ 1034
BELL DAVID DoB: 19/09/1936
E-4366961 Referrer: XXM Type: A
MRI ORBITS

REPORTED 3 1

the scan results

eye before the biopsy

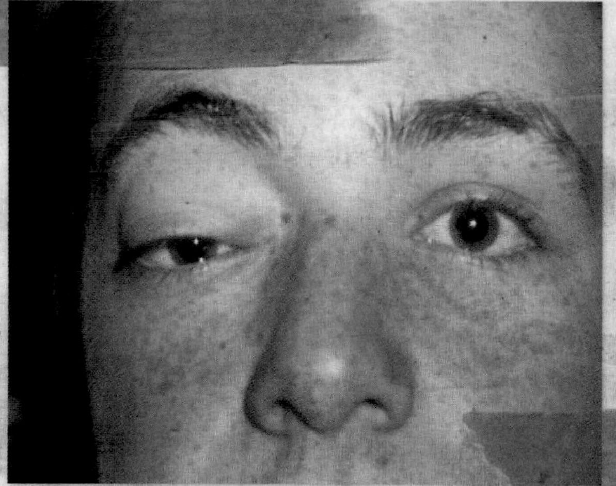

eye of
the storm...

Due to the graphic nature of the images of Dave's eye after this photo was taken, the Bell family have decided not to include those images in this section.

chemotherapy

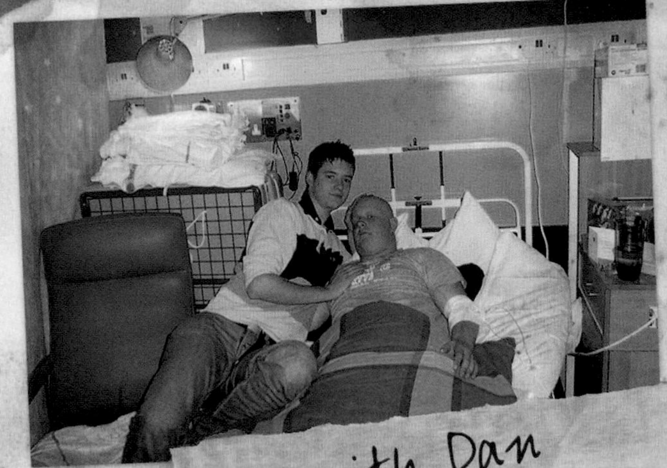

with Dan

with becki

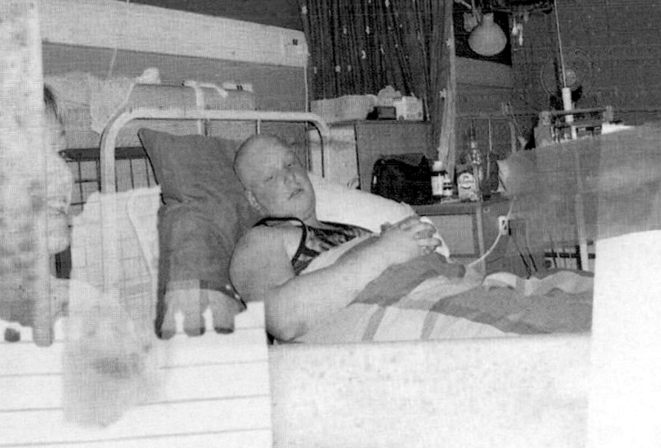

chemo takes its toll

first time out with no hair

scared,
nervous,
anxious

clamped to the table

radiotherapy

the MASK

precise alignnment

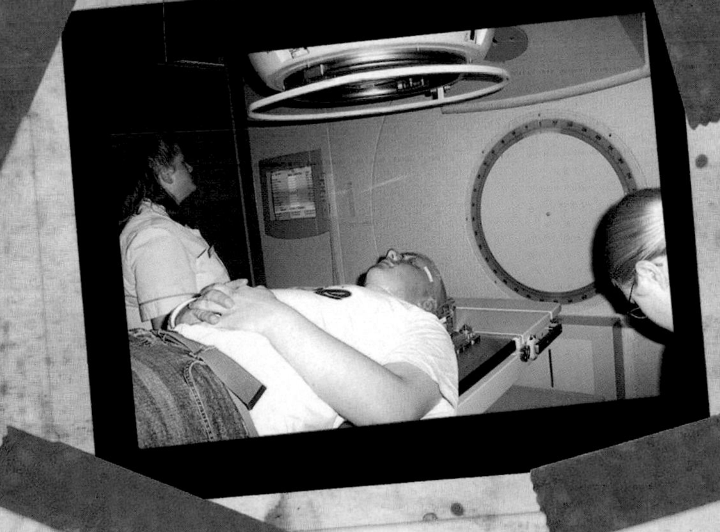

prayer

praying for healing

prayer can **change** things

with
Sir Elton John

seeing STARS

with Dad &
Eric Clapton

with
Martin Johnson
Delirious
(and Me)

the wedding

isn't she LOVELY

the boys...

ward 27
nurses

the facts

the TRUTH

the family...
These pages are dedicated to the children of Ward 27.
We ran our race together and I got to cross the finish line.
Some never got that chance.
For those children that are still running their race, I pray that you finish well.
With love, Dave. xx

lives so that we would be empowered for the new chapter that was about to open. Carpet-time was about to change to conflict-time, but what we had received would carry us through.

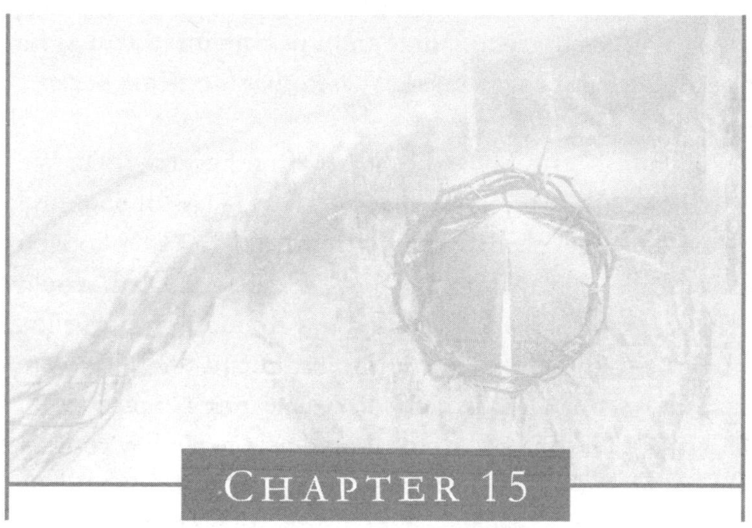

CHAPTER 15

LIGHT RELIEF

Stuart

On cloudy days the sun is often trying to break through. We know, of course, that the sun is always consistently shining, it's just that its rays are being blocked from us. During the darkest of days, shafts of light touched our world. In fact, things that had been ordinary before now became of great value. Small things took on a new meaning and we became grateful for things we had taken for granted before. I began to deeply appreciate family and friends. Sometimes the time before bed, which in the natural should have been the most difficult, took on a special meaning. David and I would sit together watching an Eric Clapton DVD and Irene would pretend that she liked the music. On other evenings David would sit and strum his guitar and I'm convinced that as he played, the darkness receded. These quiet moments became special.

Pete and Kath's house became a little haven for us. We would often pop in for a reassuring chat, a glass of wine and cheese and crackers. It's a sad statement, but I even looked forward to chewing on a stick of celery. David would disappear with Joel and Ben for a few minutes of normality. Friends became very important to us. Duane and Kris were also always there for us and of course our families stood with us. People brought us meals and helped all they could. I remember one snowy winter's day we went for a walk at 2.00am in the morning. Our faithful but confused dog, "Jazz" walked beside us and David pulled a woolly hat over his bald head as we walked around the village streets. Snow took on a new wonder.

Travelling far from Lincoln was not easy. We had to make sure that a specialist hospital was in reach if we needed any help, but we were desperate to get a break. We decided to visit some friends in Littlehampton. John and Kristen Thatcher invited us to stay in their home and these few days hold special memories for us. We did very little. We took long walks by the sea and drank coffee in seafront cafés. As Irene and I lay in bed at night we listened to the breaking waves as the tide came in. The daytimes were warm and sunny; we sat a lot and read a lot. David has never been one for sitting around and he fully entered into meeting new friends and mixing in with all their trips and activities. Delirious? kindly spent some time praying for him and offering lots of encouragement. A few days away helped us recharge before returning to the fight.

Though football was out of the question, David decided

that golf would have to fill the gap for a while. His Hickman line was fitted to allow him maximum swing. I have to confess that I was always nervous as David refused to do things by halves. He would constantly push himself and if there were any spare minutes available we would drive to the driving range to hit a few balls. His refusal to stay in contributed to a positive mindset.

Jeff Lucas always brought light and humour. It was like a tonic. David would brighten within the first few minutes of a visit. I was amazed at how colour would come to his face. I don't know what it is, but my attempts at humour would usually attract a groan, whereas one quip from Jeff would have Dave and Irene rolling in the aisles. I suppose a prophet is not without honour except in his own house! Jeff and Kay were so supportive and seemed to understand what we were going through. I welcomed Jeff's listening ear (and the rest of him as well) as I unloaded my thoughts. His sound judgment really helped me. I was deeply grateful that he visited on the morning David and I had to attend the fertility clinic. I had dreaded the appointment, but the three of us brought mirth and joy to ourselves, if not to anyone else. David faced a difficult day, but it was surrounded by light.

Jeff and Donna Summers also were light carriers. Jeff's zany humour proved a winner with David, particularly on an outing to a panto at the Theatre Royal in Lincoln where Jeff tried eagerly to engage with British humour. The result was an interesting blend of Texan line dancing with Aladdin's lamp. Jeff's shouts of, "He's behind you!" could be heard on the stage, much to the embarrassment of Donna. Laughter is good medicine.

We also experienced light moments in the Royal Infirmary (perhaps a name change would be helpful!). Our team of nurses were the best. Even routine check-ups had their lighter moments. On occasions, as David entered the consulting room, Irene and I would hear him say, "Any excuse to get my shirt off!" He also worked at building a rapport with his consultant of few words. One day he asked if he could share some things with her in confidence. He had already discussed these issues with us, but felt that by having personal time with her she would warm to him. The strategy worked and I think she had a bit of a soft spot for him. All the hospital staff were working hard for our success. We are very grateful!

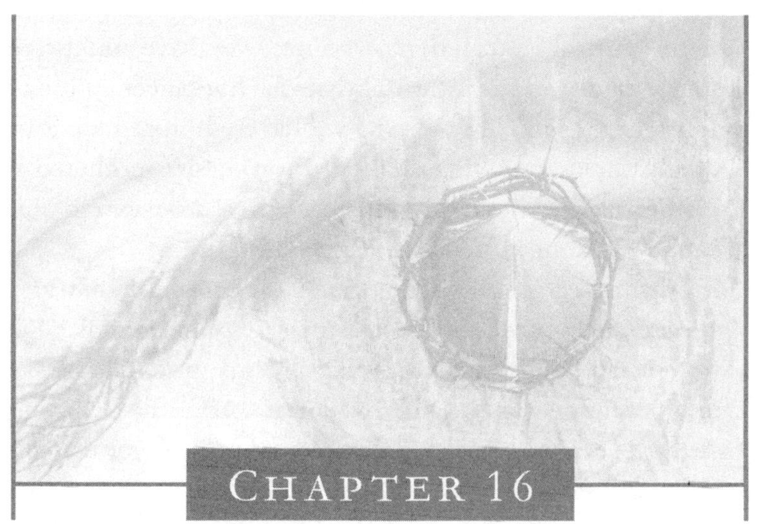

CHAPTER 16

THE FIRST CHRISTMAS

Stuart

One of our first prayer requests was, "Lord, please let it be over for Christmas!" For this to happen every treatment would have to be on time. It is highly usual that during a chemotherapy protocol of nine sessions there will be infections and therefore delays. We were told to expect this, but our focus was Christmas Day. Irene particularly has loved the Christmas season from when she was a young girl. In fact, in New Life Church she is affectionately known as Mother Christmas by those who know her best. Our house takes on grotto-like qualities for the month of December, tasteful grotto-like qualities of course. We have multi-tree displays and candles and Christmas fragrances fill our rooms. Those who are worried we have embraced a pagan festival should know that we have thoroughly smothered it in the joy of knowing that Jesus has entered our world and Irene's less subtle words are, "Get a life!"

Christmas carries happy memories for us as a family and we were determined that Christmas 2003 would not be different. So we set our faces like flint to make Christmas our target. Irene was like a rottweiler when it came to having treatments on time, whilst our consultant was eager that we had the full story and said that treatment could take up to a year if there were many delays. For some the Christmas season doesn't offer such joyful feelings, but for us we have many fond recollections. I remember spending Christmas Eve one year putting together a large Cindy-doll house for Becki. I always amazed myself at how irritated I could get when things didn't go together as easily as the instructions said they should. Andrew was a Lego genius, so my skills waited until Boxing Day when we could create a small town together. David would always receive the more active presents. One year for our morning Christmas service he insisted on going as Fireman Sam. I can see him now in his yellow helmet. I also remember the occasion when he passed Irene the phone. Apparently he had rung 999 and asked for Ponty Pandy Fire Station. The operator was not too happy. So Christmas carries fond memories for us all.

After David's first treatment, which lasted two days, he returned to Leicester a few days later for another chemo dose. He had these infusions between the main sessions in the first month. He got home as quickly as possible and went golfing with a friend. Though he was encouraged to live life as normally as possible, this was a little extreme. He overdid it and as a result ended up in hospital with a high temperature. When I received the news I was speaking in Brighton. That night I paced around my hotel room praying and declaring Scripture. If this was happening right at the beginning, was it realistic that we should focus on Christmas? After all, it wasn't essential, the main thing was that he would be fully well. However, in the morning David was out of hospital as they found nothing out of order and never had to go back for any kind of infection or problem throughout the rest of the treatment.

In the days ahead there were two further challenges to our time deadline. We learned that each course of treatment would depend on the state of David's blood. During each session his blood took a major battering and the red blood corpuscles would take time to recover. We would often ask that, "the life of God be in the blood"! On two occasions the blood levels were too low to permit the next treatment to begin. On both occasions something special took place. I will recount one of the occasions. On Bonfire Night the hospital rang to say that David would not be able to begin his next treatment in the morning as his neutrofils were at 0.7 (I have no clue what this means, but I wrote down the information as it came). Irene said that it was essential that he was not delayed and could a fresh sample of blood be taken. The nurse admired her spirit and said, "You can if you wish, but it is unlikely anything will happen overnight." Irene arranged for blood to be taken in our own doctor's surgery. The blood would be checked and the results phoned to Leicester the following morning. Irene was determined that we would not be delayed and phoned the ward as soon as she was able the following day. The nurse said, “I don’t think you’ll believe it.” Irene jumped in with the words, “Oh, I think I will!” The nurse continued, “His blood level is now 1.7.” Irene said we would come over as planned. We had a similar thing happen on another occasion and on the ward he was nicknamed, “The magical neutrofil maker”. We, however, knew that this was the work of the “Miracle Maker”. The second time the consultant asked the nurse to check to make sure it really was David’s blood, but of course it was.

Our journey continued. Perhaps I could let you know at this point that even after his first session there was a noticeable change to his eye. Our consultant encouraged us with the words, “David, this is very impressive.” The tumour had clearly reduced. The finishing date seemed to be in view. We encouraged David to keep going. The end of treatment was in sight. Then, an unexpected twist took us by surprise. Our consultant told us that though things were going very well, the latest worldwide research suggested that for this kind of tumour a course of radiotherapy was essential. Our hearts sank. This would involve twenty-five consecutive days of treatment. We would now have to make the daily drive to Nottingham, Monday to Friday.

We were aware that intensive therapy could severely damage his eye. In reality we had little choice. Irene and I rang a specialist hospital in America and even made a trip to the Middlesex Hospital in London to meet a top expert in the field. The advice was that Nottingham would do a good job for us. Would we make our deadline now? We regrouped for another phase of the battle. On Monday the 10th November we travelled to Nottingham (incidentally, all my family mock me for having meticulously kept a diary for decades now, but this eccentricity has allowed me to accurately record things that the rest of my family would have forgotten). We arrived at the reception only to be told that the special bed was broken and therefore treatment would be delayed. I fully expected Irene to get a screwdriver out of her handbag to sort things out, but thankfully it was only going to be a 24-hour delay. The next morning as fog swirled around Lincoln's streets David took his driving test and passed first time.

On the 14th November he had his treatment and we had breakfast at a Little Chef. I include this information as this is usually the kind of detail that fills my diary. Friday 28th November my entry for the day reads, "Good news on David's eye from ophthalmic specialist." At 5 o'clock on Tuesday 9th December, Becki and Glen took us to Solihull for prayer at David Carr's church. The 16th December entry reads, "Final radiotherapy session for David" and, yes, you've guessed it, on 19th December, 2003, my diary entry reads, "Last chemo session in Leicester".

Though no scan had yet been taken we were convinced of its outcome. We now began to relax as we entered into the countdown for Christmas morning. What a special Christmas it became. We went to church and were greeted by a large crowd of energetic believers. I did my normal self-indulgent session with the children as they showed off their toys and I spoke on "Light". Perhaps it was because David's eye had been my focus for many weeks. We thanked God for our miracle walk. After Christmas dinner, for me, the events of the afternoon are etched into my mind for ever. There we all were – the whole family sitting down together. I looked around the circle of contentment. By this time everyone was sleeping or close to asleep. I looked at David, his bald head revealing something of his journey. I had become used to quoting verses and a verse briefly flashed across my mind, an obscure verse in many ways: "… *and Samson's hair began to grow.*" I was conscious that David would look very different on future Christmas days. I felt very proud as I continued round the circle. Becki and Glen were both asleep, David was now snoring, Andrew and Irene were well and truly gone and even Jazz, our dog, with paws heavenward was fast asleep.

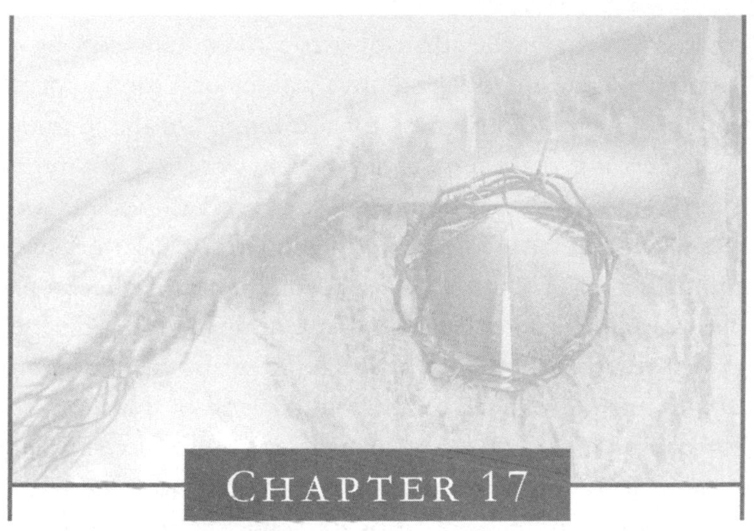

SEEING STARS

Stuart and Dave

Grace and Lanri Saidu are wonderful New Life intercessors. From the beginning they declared that David would receive "double for his trouble". They represent praying people who, with violence, are taking the Kingdom. They are intolerant towards the enemy and stand firm upon God's Word. With people like them around we feel secure. So what would "double" look like? We began to position ourselves with a sense of expectation for the future. Within a short period of time God began to open interesting doors. It felt as though we were receiving sugar to take away the bitter taste of medicine.

When all three of our children were small I dedicated an evening each week which I designated as "treat night". This could simply take the form of a trip to McDonald's or a spontaneous desire to take a drive to the coast (don't linger on the thoughts of Skegness for too long). On the journey back I would make up stories which were usually more interesting than my sermons. It now seemed as though God was saying to us, "It's now treat night." This clearly became a time of favour. On one of our regular morning check-ups our consultant said to David, "I have arranged for someone to visit you today." We learned that the celebrity in question would most likely have been afraid not to turn up as our consultant commanded considerable authority. To our surprise through the door appeared the towering figure of Martin Johnson, the captain of England's world cup rugby team. He sat by the bedside and offered a handshake that engulfed our hands one by one. I had a theory that all our hands collectively would have about filled his one hand. We were then introduced to a number of the Leicester Tigers and received tickets for a European cup match. It became obvious that a number of the team didn't know what to expect on an oncology ward. One player, seeing a bandage on David's arm, asked him if he'd broken his arm, a question that caused David some mirth. Not to be outdone, Leicester City arranged tickets for us for their next Saturday game.

One evening four representatives from the Make-a-Wish Foundation, a charity that helps children with life-threatening diseases, came to our home. They asked David to think of something he would especially like to do or a person who he would like to meet. David sat unusually quietly on the settee, unsure as to what was being offered. The team suggested that he could ask for anything as long as it wasn't £10,000 or a pool for the back garden. I could see the cogs in David's brain turning, which was actually quite an unusual event. "I'd like to meet Eric Clapton," he eventually said. He was then asked for two other possibilities if the first choice didn't work out.

From a young boy David has loved the guitar playing of Eric Clapton. I have to confess that I was also hoping to be included. A strange mixture of coincidences resulted in Eric being willing to meet David, a blessing afforded to very few. It wasn't long before first-class rail tickets to London's King's Cross arrived in the post. The package included a visit to Madam Tussauds, sight-seeing, a meal at the Hard Rock Café and two nights in a five-star hotel at the back of Harrods. Then the big evening arrived and a stretch limousine pulled up at the hotel. Staff from the hotel stood either side of the corridor sending us off as though we were royalty. The more theologically trained will, of course, know that that is exactly who we are! As we drove through London streets our posing son pulled down the window to enjoy his rock star moment.

We were taken to the doors of the Royal Albert Hall and escorted through the security. Our Make-a-Wish representative took us for a drink and, leaning across the table, said, "I do have to warn you that this is a high profile visit for us and I can't promise it will happen, even at this late stage." But within minutes the door opened and a large security man armed with large tags and bands said, "I'm going to ask you to come quickly, but I can only take two!" David and I were on our feet waving to poor Irene as we disappeared down the corridor. I wish that I could tell you that I would have been happy for Irene to go, but everyone knows this had to be a father-son moment. David and I were taken onto the Albert Hall stage and were first of all introduced to Eric Clapton's guitar technician. By his feet were racks of guitars, which he showed us one by one. This man's wife had just begun treatment for cancer and so conversation was easy. In fact, after giving David plectrums, CDs and various memorabilia he said, "I'm going to let you do something that nobody in the world has done before!" With that he picked up the famous graffiti'd Fender guitar and placed it round David's neck. "Have a play of this!" We were being showered with kindness. From the platform we were ushered into a small room where a man at the other side of a table was making a phone call. Yes, we were going to meet the legend that is known as Eric Clapton. As this was really David's treat, I'll let him continue the story.

> "From an early age, Dad and I would listen to Eric Clapton in the car on long journeys and I would watch his DVDs at night for hours whilst playing along with my guitar. The idea of meeting Eric was really a dream for me. Eric Clapton would not usually be associated as a guitar hero for a guitarist of my age, because of his style of playing and age, I presume. But I listened to him, not just because he is a great guitarist, but because he is also a remarkable songwriter. It was a great experience walking into the room and meeting him. He was a very reserved man, but friendly. He said that he was very honoured that I wanted to meet him, but then he said that he would be praying for me. Now I'm hoping that he's praying to the same God that we do, but nevertheless it was a very kind gesture!"

After Eric, came Elton. Another charity, "Wishes 4 Kids", knowing of David's love for music, arranged for us to meet Elton John in Birmingham. This day was a sweet and sour day. In fact the day began with the sour. On 29th June, 2004, at 9.30am we left for Leicester Royal Infirmary. We called into McDonald's for breakfast and then went directly for David's six-monthly MRI scan. After waiting for an hour David was becoming quite anxious. Then we were told that part of the scan had to be done again. As you can imagine, we were beginning to feel a little unsettled. But from the sour morning events we drove down to the Holiday Inn ready to begin our next adventure. We relaxed, had a swim and began to feel better. At 4 o'clock Russell from Wishes 4 Kids came to meet us in the hotel. Again we were taken in a stretch limousine along the M6 to the NEC at Birmingham. We had a meal at the restaurant and then were taken behind the scenes for an audience with Elton John. This time Irene was included and again I'll let David pick up the story from here.

> "If there is one person that I would want to meet who has been successful in the music scene, is a phenomenal musician and writes epic songs, it would be Sir Elton. We arrived at the NEC in Birmingham after a short limo ride from Leicester. For insurance purposes I had to be escorted in a wheelchair around the venue. Not my ideal form of transport, but on the other hand I got to the front of all the queues. We were taken backstage to meet some of the crew and then finally to meet the main man himself. We walked into his dressing room (which was unbelievable). I was then introduced to Sir Elton who was possibly the nicest person I have ever met. He took a genuine interest in me and spent a good amount of time with us. I was then wheeled to our seats in the arena. During the

> evening, Sir Elton dedicated the song "Philadelphia Freedom" to me. A rather funny moment came halfway through the evening when I decided that I needed the toilet. I managed to persuade Russell that the wheelchair didn't need to accompany me on this occasion, as the proceedings would be made slightly more difficult, if you know what I mean. So I got up out of the wheelchair and began to run to the toilet, only to realize that I was parked in a disabled seating area with lots of other people sat in wheelchairs. They all looked at me in disgust, thinking that I had just used the wheelchair to get some good seats! That's actually not a bad idea, come to think of it!"

I'll share just one more "treat" in this chapter. As part of a money-raising event Make-a-Wish Foundation had arranged to host a celebratory evening on Brick Lane in the East End of London. A famous French pop artist had arranged to exhibit his paintings. One morning the phone rang: "I wonder if David would be willing to be our guest at a special event in London? Perhaps he could share about his Eric Clapton visit?" We didn't have to pray about it, we were more than happy to be their guest. However, David wanting to make the most of every opportunity cheekily asked if Atlas, the band he played lead guitar for, could play at the event. "David, I can't promise that, but send us a CD and we'll see," came the answer.

In the next post David sent off a demo and waited for a response. I think even he was surprised when the organiser came back to say that not only could Atlas play, but he was willing to transport the band and offer an evening in a nice hotel in Docklands. What an amazing evening it was. We arrived at Brick Lane in a fleet of taxis. As we walked towards the entrance we heard the words, “Stand back our Make-a-Wish child has arrived.” David loved it (apart from the “child” comment). The people parted to reveal a red carpet. David, with girlfriend Sarah, walked down the carpet as cameras flashed on either side. Irene and I wandered in behind thinking, “That’s our boy!” We were shown the exhibition and David, together with Atlas, posed in front of the paintings. Atlas was the support act for the night. They did really well and before the last song David was asked to say a few words. After giving his thanks to Make-a-Wish he gave a short testimony. He said, “Two things helped me through my ordeal, my love for music and my faith in God. God has saved the day!” The audience loudly applauded. Then all the way from America, just for this one event, out came a ten-piece band and, on piano, the legendary Little Richard. David had to look on the website to see who he was, but people of my age will understand what a treat this really had become. At the end of the evening as Little Richard gave out Gospel tracts it felt as though we had been in a church meeting. Back to David to conclude the chapter.

> “Supporting Little Richard was a night that I will never forget. Gene Simmons from the band Kiss was standing in the crowd watching the band for the majority of our set. He spoke to me after the event and made some nice comments about the band and my guitar playing. The Make-a-Wish foundation really went out of their way to make our time so special. Wishes 4 Kids is the charity that lined up the Elton experience. The charity is run by a great guy called Russell who selflessly gives his time to bring glimpses

of hope into the lives of sick children. I highly commend their work.

Whilst meeting famous people doesn't really change the state or circumstances of your health, I think it certainly helps. It was something to look forward to, something to work towards. I do really believe that a wish can't change everything in a sick life, but it can change something."

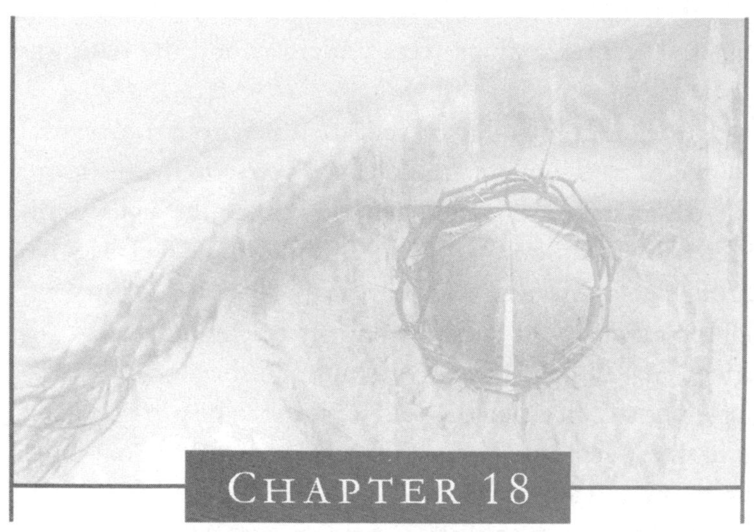

CHAPTER 18

PARTY TIME

Dave

I can remember just before the time when I started my treatment we went out to our favourite Chinese restaurant with my Godparents, Duane and Kris. We sat and listened to a small jazz band playing in the corner and we had a really great time together. On the drive home I told Mum and Dad that when this was all over I wanted to have a big celebration party which I could invite all my friends to. I had it all pictured in my head with a big band playing, formal dress, food and someone special to say a few words. This day just felt so far away, I wasn't sure if it would even arrive. This party had to be just right so I wanted all of my hair to have grown back and for me to look fairly normal again. The preparations were underway and the date was decided on.

Throughout all of my visits to the various hospitals I started to take some pictures. There were two main reasons for this. Firstly, so that I can remember throughout my lifetime what God has done for me and what He has brought me through. Secondly, to produce a DVD of my journey that would be shown at my celebration party. My friend Mat designed the invitations and they looked amazing. My sister Becki kindly paid for them to be professionally printed. When they arrived back we sent them out to everyone and anyone!

The big day eventually arrived. I was nervous for the entire week leading up to the party as I wasn't too sure what I felt about the prospect that everyone was going to be there just for me. I put my suit on, some hair wax in my brand new hair and drove down to the church feeling slightly emotional that this day actually was becoming a reality. When I arrived, the church looked unbelievable. There must have been over twenty large round tables full of decorations and there were fairy lights everywhere. I had invited all of my school friends, the nurses from Ward 27, all of my neighbours and all of my church friends. Before everyone arrived I went into one of the back rooms of the church and asked a few people to come with me to pray over the evening, primarily for all of my school friends, many of whom possibly hadn't even stepped into a church before, and for the Ward 27 nurses. I walked back into the church to find the place full of people. I was worried that no one would come! The proceedings were about to start, but there was still no sign of the nurses. I tried to delay everything by a few minutes, but ultimately we had to carry on. Halfway through the band's first song the doors at the back of the church flung open and in walked all of the nurses. The night was now complete!

The band played for a while and then we watched some video messages from some close friends that couldn't be there on the night. Steve Chalke, Delirious? and a number of American friends brought greetings. Whilst the food was being served, the famous Chris Bowater played some background jazz. Mum then got up to say a few words, slightly tearful, but her expressions were compelling and rich! She then introduced our guest speaker, Jeff Lucas. I was so proud to have Jeff and Kay there that night, not just because Jeff is a bit of a celebrity within Church circles, but he and Kay were now two of my closest friends. He did an incredible job!

Now it was time for the DVD. All of the pictures were set to a song by Delirious? called "My Glorious". I wanted people to see visually, especially school friends and even some church friends that cancer treatment isn't just a few pills, a bit of tiredness and temporary loss of hair, but is one of the most frightening, indescribable regimes in the world. The DVD that people saw that night didn't even scratch the surface of what happened in 2003, but it was a start. Many school friends were in a state of shock once the pictures had finished and many were reduced to uncontrollable tears. People just didn't know what it was like. Later in the evening my Dad got up and introduced the Ward 27 nurses. A standing ovation, ripples of applause and even a few cheeky wolf whistles from the "lads" at the back came from the crowd as they walked out to the front to receive some presents and flowers. The night was coming to an end; however, there was one final thing to be done. There was a guitar lying on the stage that had my name on it and a full band just waiting for me to strike the first chord of *Johnny B. Goode*. As soon as I started to sing, many first-time commitments were made . . . unfortunately not to the Lord Jesus!

Guests began to leave and a team of friends started the big clear-up process. It had been the night I had longed for. It felt good to be alive.

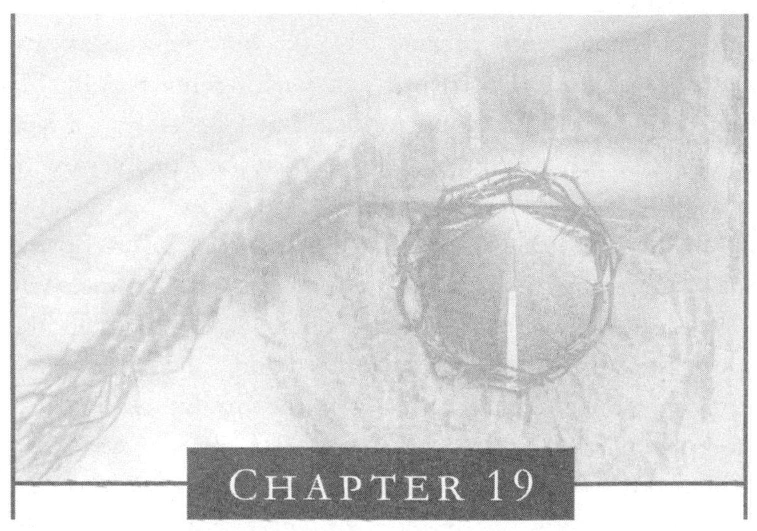

Chapter 19

Sweet Sarah

Dave

When you stare into a hospital mirror to see the reflection of a bald, pale, overweight cancer patient staring back at you, the idea of someone ever loving you is a dream you don't think can ever be a reality. When I was ill I could never imagine looking how I used to look or even my eye returning to how it was. I had to prepare myself for the fact that I may not have a right eyebrow or any eyelashes on my right eye and could even have some deformity to the bone structure in my face. The idea of having a girlfriend was a distant one. It was somewhere in the back of my mind, but considering the circumstances, I never really entertained the idea. I just assumed that no one would be attracted to me. When out with friends I would, on some occasions, remain quiet in the corner just wearing my woolly hat and hoping no one would notice that I had rather a lack of hair for the average sixteen-year-old or a problem with my eye.

In the summer of 2004, Duane and Kris White hosted "Launch" which was a youth missions programme. The week of training was held in Lincoln and then all the delegates were sent out across the world. I hadn't planned on going, but after a few chats with the Godfather I decided to book in at the last minute. One possible motive was that I knew there could be a few girls going and I think that swayed me. For one reason or another I was late for registration so I went straight to the evening meal. I walked into the room and had a quick look around to see lots of new faces, but then time stood still. Over in the corner was sitting what can only be described as "one hot unit". To all of our foreign readers this terminology can only be translated as "one hot unit"! I immediately assumed that she must be American or live miles away from me. I plucked up the courage to go over and speak to her later on that night. I asked her name and where she was from expecting to hear an American accent. "Sarah," she quietly replied with an English accent, "from Grimsby," she added. Hold the phone ... Grimsby? That's only forty minutes away from Lincoln. I did begin to think, "Surely something this pretty could not have come from Grimsby." This was too good to be true. I later realized that we had both been to Grapevine for the last sixteen years and never seen one another. She had also been to an Atlas concert, but I never saw her there either.

Sarah was going on a missions trip to Kenya and I wasn't,

so I asked her if I could come and see her when she got back. Her reply wasn't really what I was after, but in a roundabout way she eventually said that I could. The day arrived and I managed to convince Dad that it would help my cause if I picked her up in his Audi. We spent the day together, but eventually it was time for me to leave. I tried to linger before getting back into the car to see if I was going to get a little kiss, but she wasn't having any of it! I told her that I liked her and to my surprise she said she liked me too. I thought the whole "... as a friend" speech was going to follow, but it didn't. I was in there!

The next time we met was at the Grapevine set-up week where I offered my services in the white-lining department. This was only because Sarah was doing it, I wasn't really interested in white-lining in all honesty. This is where the first embarrassing story comes in. Sarah and I were walking towards the exhibition centre one afternoon only to find a massive pool of water blocking the entrance. Any normal person would possibly use a different entrance or try in some way to avoid the large quantity of muddy water, but no, not me. I had to try and act cool in front of Sarah, so I decided to attempt to leap over the water. I went for it but gravity took effect quicker than I had calculated. I not only landed in the centre of what could only be described as a full-on pond, but had to reach across to Sarah to stop me from fully submerging as I had lost all sense of balance. Sarah's overall physique is slightly different from mine in that she weighs about half what I do, so you can picture her attempting to hold me up. I don't easily get embarrassed, but this occasion made my cheeks a little bit red. On the final night of Grapevine, Sarah and I started going out ... good times.

The Engagement

Three years later I decided that it was time for me to think about asking "the question". I can remember talking to Mum and Dad and saying that I was going to ask Sarah's Dad if I could marry his daughter. I was slightly nervous that Dave (Sarah's dad) was going to ask me some in-depth spiritual and biblical questions on marriage, so I got Dad to give me some possible answers to overcome this possible problem. I was all set!

The night that I decided I was going to ask him, well, put it this way, I've never been so nervous in all my life! I walked in and out of his office about six times before I even said a word! Eventually, I stopped being a girl and asked him the question. He asked me in a stern voice, "Give me three good reasons why you should marry my daughter." Not really the kind of response I had planned in my head. I was thinking more along the lines that a simple "yes" would suffice. So I started to stutter that I believed that God had brought us together and we could accomplish more together than apart (I thought I would ease him in with a little Christian viewpoint, just to warm him up). I then quoted the Bible stating that it was better to marry than to burn in passion. Thanks for that one, Dad, it worked a treat! Before I started the third he stopped me and said, "Yes, of course you can marry my daughter." He then prayed for me and gave me his blessing, which I thought was an amazing thing. The next Grapevine was the time that I had chosen to propose. It was the last day of the event and I had arranged for a team of people to help me decorate some of the gardens. I had a big archway full of fairly lights and candles everywhere. Leading from the archway was a little gazebo with champagne, chocolates and our favourite song playing. I put on my suit and waited for her under the archway. It had all gone to plan. She arrived without knowing a thing.

The Wedding

For most people of my age, talking about marriage would be quite straightforward, you either get married or you don't. I had to have a conversation with Sarah that most people would never have to have, especially not someone of my age. We had to talk about the facts again, the possibility of not being able to have children. I felt quite worthless and ashamed of actually having to say these words to her and to someone who has a big love of children. But when somebody tells you that it doesn't make her feel any different and she still loves you the same, that is an amazing thing. We believe that this prospect is only a *fact*. The *truth* is that God can turn this situation around for His glory and we will be able to have children.

The wedding plans were underway and this distant dream was nearly in reach. The big day arrived. Throughout this book I have usually referred to the "big day" or the "epic day" as something awful dawning, but not this time. This is the day that, against all the odds, I was going to get married. I had four best friends as best men. My dad, my brother Andrew, my brother-in-law Glen and my cousin Ben. In addition to this I had ten of my closest friends as ushers (slightly excessive but who cares!). Sarah had five bridesmaids and two little flower girls.

All the best men and ushers lined up at the back of the church. I looked out onto a massive crowd of people. It was unbelievable. The music came on and we all walked down in a row to the *Top Gun* theme tune. Can you guess whose idea that was? I wrote the piece of music that Sarah was to walk down the aisle to. Me being me, I did it the night before, not the best idea in the world. The music started to play and one by one the bridesmaids walked down. Finally, the moment arrived when I saw Sarah. Words couldn't describe how beautiful she looked. My eyes started to fill up as I thought about the fact that this was real life, not a dream.

Dad had a few roles that day. Not only was he my best man, but he also married us. The ceremony began and I was doing well until he spoke the line, "... in sickness and in health". I had to pause and fight back the tears. This line was a struggle. The reception was held at the Lincolnshire Show Ground. This was an amazing venue for us as this was the place that we first started going out and it was also the place where we got engaged.

Looking back, this was one of the best days of my life. I didn't want it to end. Nearly a year on, Sarah and I have an amazing house and are so thankful for all that we have. I do feel slightly sorry for Sarah on some occasions, because I do act like a twelve-year-old the majority of the time. Recently, my little brother-in-law Josh had his thirteenth birthday party. This was an ideal time for me to get away with doing rather immature things. They somehow convinced me to play "knock and run" for the majority of the evening. It didn't really take much convincing in all honesty. But later it dawned on me and I had to stop and think, "Dave, you're twenty-one, married, and you're playing "knock and run" with a bunch of thirteen-year-olds!" Another good example of this happened quite recently when Sarah and I went to Mum and Dad's house for a drink with a few of their friends. Sarah stayed inside by the fire chatting with everyone like a normal person. I, however, was outside sitting in the tree house that I had built (I said that I had built it for my little nephew, Jermac, but it was really for me) shooting pigeons with a bb gun. I am so thankful that Sarah has that more adult nature that I am certainly lacking, because she keeps me out of trouble!

Sarah, you have made my life complete and I thank God for you every day. I could never imagine someone loving me with the titles that I have over my life, but you have looked past all of these. Thank you for loving me just how I am. You are my best friend and I love every second I have with you. I believe that when God enters a situation He doesn't leave it half finished. This can only mean that one day we will have children together and that's when a new chapter of our lives is written.

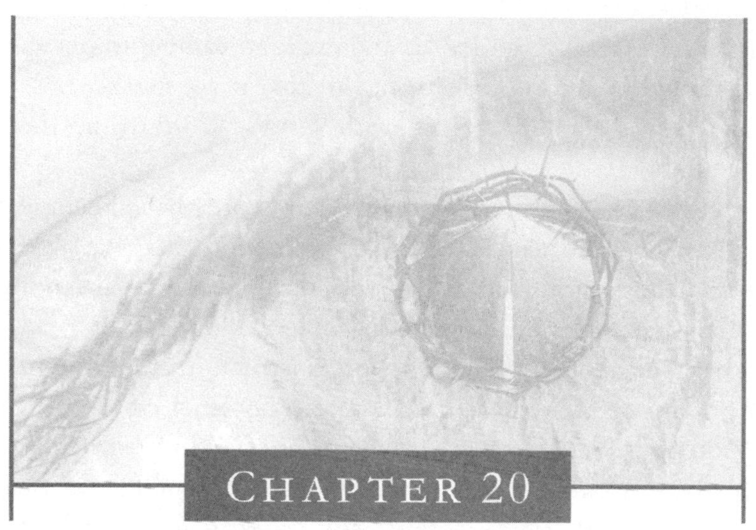

CHAPTER 20

FACTS OR TRUTH?

Stuart and Dave

Words are very powerful. They can carry the light of heaven or be like rockets fuelled by hell. The book of Proverbs assigns great power to words. Proverbs 18:21 says, *"The tongue has the power of life and death, and those who love it will eat its fruit."* Speaking the truth of God's Word is what the tongue was originally designed for. We need to fill the air with good words, positive and life-giving words, words of encouragement, strengthening and healing. When we are praised or built up we stand up on the inside and find ourselves able to face life with certainty.

Words spoken by God are words of life: *"By faith we understand that the universe was created by the word of God"*

(Hebrews 11:3). God spoke and creation came into being. It should therefore not surprise us that if we speak words of life we align ourselves with God's Word from the beginning.

However, we live in a world where words have become compromised. Instead of clear words of trust we find ourselves surrounded by mixed messages. We are not sure where we stand or what people really mean or what they think about us. The following instructions were found on items in some shops in England. A label on a bread pudding read, *"Product will be hot after heating"*, the instruction label on a child's cough medicine bottle stated, *"Do not drive car or operate machinery"*, and a particular brand of peanuts was labelled *"Warning – contains nuts"*. We become confident when communication is clear and filled with faith, but we soon struggle when we are not sure what has been said.

Many people today live with a sense of low self-worth because of the power of words in their lives, often from childhood days. If a teacher declares that we are useless at a particular subject we find it difficult to believe otherwise. Other people actually endorse their own weaknesses with words like, "I'm no good" or "I'll never change". Too often the first words in a conversation are, "You've put weight on!" or "You don't look well," rather than an affirmation of a person's good points. These principles become even more important when speaking of health issues. If someone says to us that we are "looking pale" it's not long before we begin to feel unwell. Of course, I am not suggesting that we live in a world where we don't face facts, but increasingly we need to become "Word" orientated rather than be guided by feelings. Faith is not denying the facts, but it is exalting the truth. As the power of the Word increases in our thinking, so the truth of the Word begins to operate and the truth brings us into God's realm of freedom. Romans 8:31 asks the question, *"What then shall we say in response to this?"* Paul has just outlined the truth of God's unfailing love and care that works for the believer's total good. The answer is clear, *"If God is for us, who can be against us?"* He goes on to say that though trouble and pressure will come our way we can stand in total confidence of God's love. In fact nothing at all will be able to separate us from the love of God that is in Christ Jesus our Lord (Romans 8:39).

Now let's get back to the story. When we are confronted with bad news we can quickly feel shaken and challenged. On hearing that David had cancer we found that our imaginations ran haywire. The roots of our belief systems were tested big time and we had to make choices. As a Christian minister I was aware that in a fallen world bad things happen to everyone at times. I knew that I must wholeheartedly trust God and not give any room to unbelief, but I was also aware that I must not enter the unreal world of denial. Initially, I felt floored by the news, but the Scriptures I had known from boyhood soon came to my rescue. I thought of the healing ministry of Jesus and of the fact that Jesus Christ the Son of God came into the world to destroy the devil's work. There was no doubt in our minds that this was the devil's work, so on a daily basis as a family we filled our minds with truth. We confessed healing every day and sent a daily prayer outline to all our friends and intercessors.

When people who are in authority make statements, their words carry incredible weight. This is especially true in the field of medicine. Doctors and consultants are rightly recognised as having expert knowledge in their particular field. When they tell us what is likely to happen we assume that it is the truth. However, where health and healing is concerned there can be a higher authority at work. God is a God of miracles and when we pray we are no longer in the realm of what normally happens. A doctor may well tell us what usually happens, but the first report is not always the final report.

When we received the first report regarding David the language used was "this is very serious ... you will have a very hard time ... you will have infections ..." etc. All of these things are what would normally be expected, but a consultation where little positive news is given can be very difficult to bear. Doctors, of course, cannot just give well-meaning words, especially in days of increased levels of litigation. We learned to listen to the facts, politely nod, and then take hold of God's Word. This involved battles of the mind and the imagination. We began to learn that faith is far more than imagining things will change. It is holding on to the promises of God even when *nothing* seems to change. During these days the Scriptures became more powerful and wonderful to us. We were also aware that our prayer times were more regular and most car journeys began with intercessory prayer. It's amazing, but often pressure brings the best out in us. We were particularly sustained through our church prayer meetings and we started to look forward to them. We also made sure that each Sunday morning we requested that the elders should anoint David with oil. In the evening our prayer team set to work interspersing prayers with the promises of God.

Our experience with radiotherapy gives a great illustration of exalting the truth over the facts.

Facts:

- May have permanent loss of eyebrows
- May lose eyelashes
- May need cataract operation
- May have deformity to face
- May have pituitary gland damage
- May have damage to tear ducts
- May have curly hair

Armed with the above facts our prayer team regularly went down the list declaring the truth of God's healing power.

Truth:

- Eyebrows returned
- Eyelashes returned
- No cataract operation
- No deformity of face
- Continued physical growth
- Tears produced
- Hair colour and condition back to normal

Out of all these prayer issues our only disappointment was that David did have to have a cataract operation. We are grateful to God that many of the facts turned out not to be the truth. The first report gave the possibility of loss of sight. The last report received was with a new senior doctor who, looking into the back of both of David's eyes said, "Now David, remind me, which eye was it that you had the problem with?" You can imagine how good it was to hear those words.

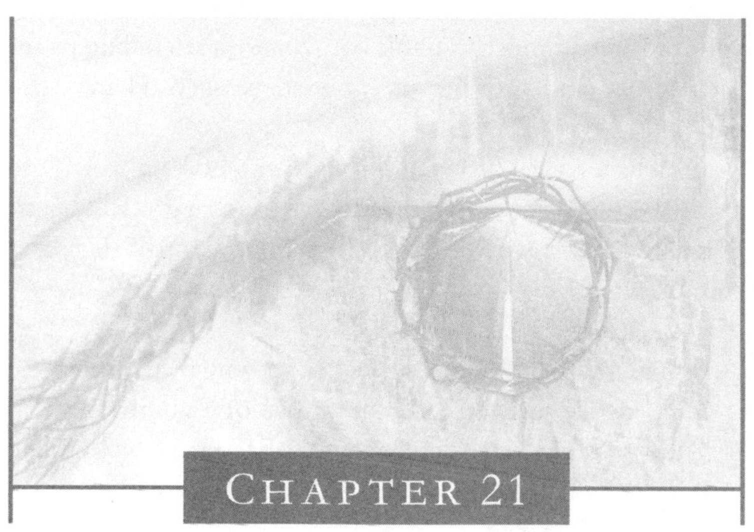

I Can Only Imagine

Irene

I thought it might be good as David's Mum, also known as Florence, to add a few of my own thoughts. Those who know me will not be surprised that I am crying already. "How can a mother go through a journey like this?" some would ask, but our family and friends, my incredible husband and of course the Miracle Maker made it possible. David showed maturity, his faith became stronger and compassion for the people around him was always there. Thank you, David, for being an example to us all. Thank you, Andrew, Becki and Glen for letting us concentrate on your brother so much. Thank you, Stuart, for guiding us on the journey and carrying us when necessary. Thank you, Sarah, for loving David.

Sometimes at night when I walked the hospital corridors alone, I would sing to myself and with such a grateful heart, wondered how I would thank God. The words of this song sum up what I feel:

> "Surrounded by Your glory what will my heart feel?
> Will I dance for You Jesus or in awe of You be stilled?
> Will I stand in Your presence or to my knees will I fall?
> Will I sing hallelujah, will I be able to speak at all?
> I can only imagine."

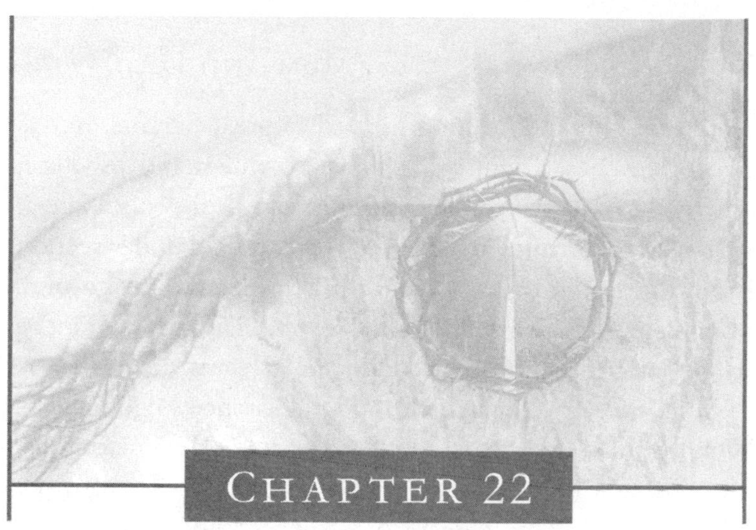

CHAPTER 22

A MILLION THANK YOU'S

Dave

To some readers this section of the book may seem irrelevant, but to me this chapter is very important. On the other hand, this is my book, so I can pretty much write what I like!

It is an unusual thing in this day and age for a teenager to have an amazing relationship with family members, especially parents. I am so thankful to God for the relationship that I have with my family and friends and for all that they have done for me.

Reeno and Stu . . . (Mum and Dad!)

I not only think of Mum and Dad as great parents, but as two of my best friends. We have so much fun together, whether it is me storming into Mum and Dad's room late at night and performing a citizen's arrest on Dad under section five of the public order act and thrusting him to the ground, or whether it's using Mum's claustrophobia to my advantage by getting her in a headlock until she screams!

Mum quickly adopted the name "Florence Nightingale". Well, I named her that, as she took on the role of caring for me. She was fully trained in how to take blood from the Hickman line. Now that, people, is a scary thought.

From an early age Dad would spend hours playing football with me, even after long days at work. In his busy schedule he always made time for me for which I am very grateful. Dad is actually a funny lad in many strange ways. If he was travelling towards the Humber Bridge he would have his toll money ready on the M25, four counties too early in my opinion. One night he and I went for a late night drive together. Stu started to reverse the car down the drive whilst looking slightly puzzled, as if something was not quite right. Still bemused, he pulled over and asked me if I thought the headlights looked dim. I stated that they looked fine. Then he turned to me and asked me if I was sure. To my amazement, he had only gone and put his darkest sunglasses on instead of his normal glasses! "No wonder it looks dark, Stu," I said, "It's 11 o'clock at night and you're wearing sunglasses!"

Ordering from a McDonald's drive through is priceless when it's Dad's turn to order. He suddenly becomes all edgy. His hand starts to nervously tap on the side of the door and his head starts to rock backwards and forwards. He will then ask for something completely random that has never ever appeared on a McDonald's menu before. For example, "drinking chocolate" – what's that?

All joking aside, Dad and Mum are the most generous people I know. There is only one person I will listen to when it comes to health and my future and that is my Dad. If you want to see a visual representation of what Dad did for me you need to watch the Rick Hoyt Story, which shows how a father carried his son through a time of trial to victory. All he needs to say are those simple words, "Every little thing is going to be alright" and then I know that all is well. Mum and Dad I love you both and thank you for making my journey a lot easier than it could have been.

Becki, Glen, Jermac and Trenton

Becki did her best to keep the family politically correct by marrying a black man, Glen. Becki and Glen never missed one visit when I stayed in hospital. Often Becki would lie beside me whilst I was having my treatment. She has never been short of words so she did keep me thoroughly entertained. She would usually try to make me play the "would you rather" game. Becki expressed her inner thoughts within poems and short letters to me. I have included a section of one of these below. Being around Becki and Glen would often result in lots of fun and laughter. When the news came that Becki was pregnant I became very excited, but at the same time thoughtful. It symbolized to me that a new life was starting, a new perspective, the next stage of my life. Life was going to change again, but this time for the better. Becki and Glen are amazing parents to Jermac and Trenton and I love spending time with them. I can remember going to watch Becki and Glen dancing in big concerts and being so proud that they were in my family. Jermac and Trenton are two of the cutest boys I have ever seen. I think that they inherited their looks from Uncle Dave. Becki, Glen, Jermac and Trenton, thank you for all you have done for me. I love being a part of your growing family.

A section of Becki's poem read:

"As I watch you face this with such strength and grace
I'd like to take it all away, the pain I would erase
But God has a purpose – it will all slot into place
For He sees the big picture and all the trials we have
to face."

Andrew (Teacher of the Year 2007)

Throughout my treatment I believe that Andrew felt a role of responsibility to uphold as the oldest child in the Bell family. He needed to be there to support my parents, but also his little brother and younger sister. This is not an easy thing to do, but Andrew took on this challenge and showed a fighting nature that is not usually associated with his character. As I mentioned in previous chapters, Andrews's disposition is rather different from mine, for which I am very grateful. Andrew would revise for an exam two years before he was due to take it. I, on the other hand, would revise for about thirty minutes on the night before. When buying a car, Andrew would be more attracted to the vehicle's fuel efficiency and depreciation costs, but I would be interested in its 0–60 time and whether the chicks would dig it!

On a more serious note, Andrew would often send me cards containing Bible verses and they would always state how proud he was of me. I have included what Andrew wrote in one of the many cards he sent me below. I have always been proud of my brother too, but this reached a whole new level recently. Andrew has always been an exceptional teacher and has often been commended through various organizations for his work. In 2007 Andrew was nominated for the prestigious award of "Primary School Teacher of the Year" at a national level. As a family we sat anxiously in the London Palladium waiting to see who had won. The Spice Girls' manager, Nicki Chapman, called out Andrew's name informing us that he had won! I was so proud to be his little brother that day.

Thank you, Andrew, for being the big brother that most little brothers want. Thank you for all your love and support. And also thank you for doing all of my English coursework.

Andrew's card read:

> "I really can say don't worry, because I know that God is saying it too, and He knows best. He will be with you and bring you through because He's already been there! So relax and let everyone look after you."

Sarah

I know that during all my treatment we were not yet a part of each other's lives and in a way I am thankful for that. I wouldn't have wanted you to see me in that way. One of the words spoken over me was "double for your trouble". I really believe that you are a part of that prophetic word over my life. I am so grateful that you believe in me and I am looking forward to us sharing life together out loud.

Sarah's Family

I want to thank Dave and Anna for allowing me to marry their beautiful daughter. You have welcomed me into your family and made me feel a part of it in every way possible. I will always be thankful for the great wedding that you provided for us. I have always wanted a little brother to play with, so Emily fits the bill nicely! All jokes aside, Emily is the best sister-in-law. She is so much fun to be around. Then there's Josh, the youngest in the family. I'm not convinced that my influence on Josh has been entirely of a good nature, however, he seems to think so! Josh is the ideal little brother.

Extended Family

After speaking with a lot a friends, especially those that don't really have a church background, I often notice that there is usually division or conflict between extended family members. I am proud to say that within my wider family that is certainly not the case. I would like to thank the Bells, the Hemsleys, the Middletons, the Cresseys and the Ross's for their encouragement and support.

Grandparents

The close nature of all of our family members is primarily down to our Grandparents. My Grandparents paved the way for our family, specifically relating to church and church life. My Granddad Bell was a preacher and was renowned for his often rather prolonged prayers. When staying overnight at their house I would usually be asleep before he had finished the eighth point of his night-time prayer. I will never forget the night when all our family gathered around to say our goodbyes to Granddad. I was young at the time, but I remember how he prayed for us and blessed us as individuals. Grandma Bell was the traditional Grandma who was always active and busy around the house, but she was never too busy for her grandchildren. I loved going round to her house to have a quick go on her Stannah stair lift!

I was too young to remember too much about my Grandma Richardson and sadly I don't have memories of her when she was well. All my information about her when she was well is contained in photos. I do know that she was a great woman. Granddad Richardson was a great friend to me. He was a brave soldier in the Second World War and perhaps I inherited his DNA, which helped prepare me for my battle in terms of courageousness. We played golf together and he would always come and watch me in my football matches. He didn't quite make it to Sarah's and my wedding. Looking back now it is upsetting that there were no grandparents on my side of the family at the wedding, but in all honestly I think God would let them have a few minutes out of their busy schedule in heaven to come and have a little look. Thank you for laying strong foundations for my success.

Duane and Kris (the Godparents!)

I think it is quite accurate to say that I have the best Godparents in the world. I must begin to annoy people because I do mention it on many occasions. The White family put their life on hold just for me, for which I will never be able to say thank you enough. Duane and Kris's youngest daughter, Ashton, would draw pictures for me and even made me a radiotherapy countdown chart. I still carry one of Ashton's notes in my wallet to this day. Cody and I would play football together for hours. I loved having Cody around and I quickly adopted him as my new little brother. I have seen Kelsey grow from being a quiet young girl to a beautiful young woman who puts God and church at the centre of her life. I am proud to know you, proud that you are my family and thank you for allowing me to be a part of yours. I love you all.

Jeff and Kay

Jeff has shared some experiences with me which no other man will ever experience. As you will have read in this book, Jeff helped me on many occasions to dig out the funny aspects of certain challenges. If there are two people that can lift someone's spirits it's Jeff and Kay Lucas. Thank you for being there for me. That little phone call that took place nearly five years ago still applies now: "I love you both."

Prayer Team

I want to thank every member of the prayer team that so faithfully prayed with me from start to finish. We had some great times together. I put prayer at the forefront of each day even if I didn't feel like it. From the outset I realized the importance of prayer and how situations can instantaneously change through the prayers of committed people. Thank you for standing with me and believing for my breakthrough. I would personally like to thank Pete and Kath Atkins who visited me on a weekly basis to pray for me. I would also like to thank Carol Backhouse for driving Mum and me to and from the majority of my radiotherapy appointments.

Ward 27 Nurses

As I mentioned in the introduction to this book, I believe that my healing was a combination of the medical profession and God's grace and provision. To be a nurse on Ward 27 is not an easy line of work. It takes a very special person to be in that atmosphere day in and day out. Every day seeing new little smiles change over a period of time to little faces of pain, confusion and hopelessness, they are the unsung heroes of our lives. I became good friends with a lot of the nurses on the ward and they often kept me entertained, especially Pauline. I think Pauline liked me a bit too much. She often tried to sneak a little grab of my bum when I was walking past or have a little squeeze of my muscles when checking my blood pressure.

In addition to this I would like to thank the oncology, radiotherapy and ophthalmology consultants that have played their part in my healing.

Friends

I am very conscious that so many friends helped out in some way or another throughout my treatment, for which I am eternally grateful, but a few names stand out of the crowd who I would personally like to thank. Firstly, Thom Law. Thom was one of the very few if not the only person that regularly called me throughout my treatment. His timing was unbelievable. Before any major procedure, scan, treatment or operation the phone would always ring with Thom saying that he was thinking about me and praying for me. He would even call after the event had taken place just to see how it went. He would remember each date and contact me without prompting on every occasion. Secondly, I would like to thank Joel Atkins. Joel and I grew up together and even reached the heights of the local village newspaper together as the unnamed youths who were responsible for a local misdemeanour. It is always the pastor's sons that you have to watch out for. Joel visited me every time I had to go into hospital. He would pack his little rucksack, get on the train from Lincoln to Leicester and walk to the hospital, just to see me. Joel never missed a visit and always came at his own expense. I can remember one time that Joel was on the train on his way to see me when I was released from hospital early. He ended up getting off the train just to get back into Dad's car to drive home.

I am very conscious that a number of others came over to visit during one of my many stays in hospital for which I am very grateful.

It is in times of trial when you realize who your friends actually are. The two friends that I have mentioned above are examples of what a true friend really is. A true friend is someone who will stick with you through the easy and the hard times. Thank you to all my friends who stuck with me and helped guide me through the storms.

International Friends

I am very fortunate to have great friends, not only in the UK, but also across the world. Mum and Dad's closest friends, Jack and Trish Groblewski, live in Bethlehem, Pennsylvania. Jack's church prayed for me constantly throughout my treatment, but it was a few weeks into my treatment when we noticed what I would call "angels", who wrote me cards for every stage of the journey. Linda and Elmer Brown would send me words of encouragement after every major milestone. The amazing thing was, every picture on the front of the card was so applicable to the situation I was in. It was remarkable. The final card that they sent was just days after I had finished my final course of treatment. It had an illustration of a cartoon character on the front taking a bow. Inside the card read:

> "Thank you for allowing us to be in a small way a part of your incredible journey. Take a bow for you and the Lord."

Francois and Ansa van Nierkerk and the South African prayer team constantly prayed for me and kept in touch with Mum and Dad. Thank you for standing with me regardless of our geographical locations.

God

In my wedding speech I saved this section till last, so I thought I would do the same in the book. If it were not for God I would not have an amazing family. If it were not for God I would not have a beautiful wife. If it were not for God I would not have a right eyebrow or eyelashes. If it were not for God I would not have a right eye. If it were not for God I would not have the chance to live the rest of my life. If it were not for God I wouldn't have hope in life or hope for the future. Thank you, God, for saving the day for me.

I have included below the bridge of a song that I wrote called "Flying Away" which really sums up what I am trying to say.

"All I can say, and all we have sung
Is to say thank you, my friend, thank you for all you
    have done
All I can say, and all we have sung
Is to say thank you, my friend, the battle is won…

After reading through this chapter it felt like I was looking at the scrolling credits at the end of a film or even a play. To be honest it could be viewed in a very similar way. These are all the people who have had starring roles or taken part in my journey. Some people were just behind the scenes in prayer ready for the next chapter and some people were at the heart of every element. Thank you for all you have done for me and for the parts you played during my treatment, but most of all, thank you to the Director of this journey, Jesus Christ.

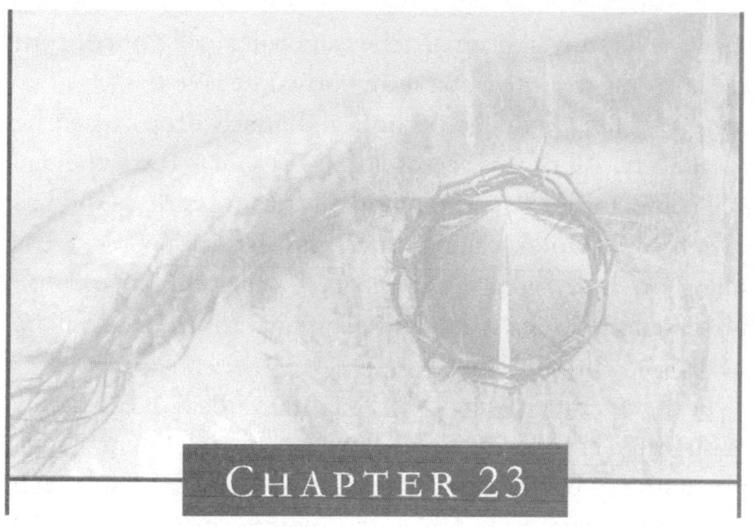

CHAPTER 23

SO WHAT'S NEXT?

Dave

Fear comes knocking at my door most days. Some days the sound of the knocking is deafening and some days it is a little fainter. I am believing that as time passes the sound will change until other sounds dominate my thinking. I look to the day when the volume will be turned up and I can live life out loud in complete freedom. I need to learn how to take my thoughts captive and bring them under the authority of God's Word.

I have to realize on a daily basis that I can face all of the facts, but I have to learn to embrace the truth. I believe that one day I will be able to read certain news stories and see documentaries without feeling uneasy and nervous. I believe that one day any abnormal aches and pains will not concern me and drag me into a spiral of worry. I believe that one day my eye will be completely whole and hourly drops won't be a necessity. All of this seems so far-off, but I know the day will come. I want to press into all the promises that God has over my life. God is calling me to pray for sick people, He is filling my heart with compassion. I believe that God has promised that when I sing and play guitar that people will be healed.

I can remember going out for a meal with all of the family about three months after I had finished my treatment. There was nothing special about where we went and it wasn't even a special occasion. It was just a normal night where the family had got together. We all sat around a large table chatting about life and what we had all done in the last week. I held little Jermac on my knee and began to look around, and that's when it hit me. I started to imagine that I was staring into a family photo of this very occasion only to notice that I was not in the picture. I mentally zoomed out from the image to see if I was the one taking the picture . . . but it was not me. It was at this moment that I realized what this date in time could have looked like. I held onto Jermac and started to cry with un-containable tears. Everyone turned to see if I was OK. I tried to explain, as much as I could, what I was feeling and how there was nothing wrong with me, but I was just so happy to be alive. Life seemed so precious and I didn't want to miss a second of it.

Recently Sarah and I went to Spain to visit her grandparents. This is when I realized that I had become, well in a way, a bit of an old man. I would still do all the usual things like swimming and showing off my muscles by the pool, but more than often I would find myself sitting on the balcony just staring at the scenery. This is strange for someone who can't keep still for longer than thirty seconds. I would sit there for hours without moving and without speaking, just looking at the mountains and all of the wildlife. I would literally stay there for the majority of the day. I had a brand new perspective on certain parts of life that I used to take for granted. I was just so thankful to be alive and to look out onto God's incredible creation. Not only that, but to see all of this with both eyes. However, I couldn't stay this calm and sentimental for too long, so I decided to send a postcard to Mum and Dad stating that I had joined the Foreign Legion, got a few tattoos and was currently writing from a Spanish prison where I was sharing a cell with my new little Spanish friend, Carlos. I thought this was hilarious and I was hoping to get the call from Mum and Dad concerned for their son's safety, but I think they know my immature nature too well by now, so they didn't call!

I have to deal with many emotions on the other side of this battle. Mainly fear, but surprising to most, a heavy weight of guilt. Guilt? I can hear you all think, but if you carry on reading you will begin to understand why. As I visit the hospital for check-ups I see little children in the same condition, if not worse, from the time when I first started my treatment. This means that some small children have been on that ward for the last three or four years of their lives and every day is a constant battle for survival. Some children have lost limbs and now have to face the rest of their life with restrictions and abnormality. Some little children just walked into that ward only to be carried out after a few months ready for a funeral. But then there is me. I am well. I feel guilty that I am the one who is disease free. I am the one who has a positive future. Some things are so hard to understand. Of course, in reality, guilt is too strong a word, but I feel humbled by the whole experience.

Back to the title of this chapter, "So What's Next?" As you will have read in the previous chapters, music and sport were the two main passions in my life before I entered this uncharted territory. For obvious reasons sport had to take a back seat in my life for a while, so I concentrated more on music. I attended an Access to Music college in the September after I finished my treatment and enrolled on a session musician's course. I had a great guitar teacher called Nige, who really helped in raising the bar in my personal music theory and overall level of musicianship. I somehow managed to pass the course with a distinction and this time it was entirely down to my own doing – except I did make Andrew type a few of my dissertations!

A kind friend of the family helped me to get a really great job within a construction company, quite diverse from music, but I looked at the possible career paths within the company and thought that I would give it a go. I was employed as a trainee contracts manager and started on a very good wage. This enabled me to get a mortgage, furnish the new house and to drive a nice car. With the nature of the construction industry I was up and down the country most days. A year on, my possible options for progressing within the company would have meant a move away from Lincoln, so I ended up leaving a well paid job, just days before I got married, to set up a new business. Pure craziness!

Throughout my life I have always been a bit of an entrepreneur and had a fascination with the business world, but I just assumed that I was too young or under-qualified to start any form of business. I listened to some teaching by a highly successful businessman by the name of Paul Milligan who stated that a business dream without action is just a fantasy. I had dreamed all of these things but never took action upon them. So I went for it and started the business even when the circumstances suggested otherwise. Marshall & Bell Ltd was incorporated and officially started trading in September 2007. The "Marshall" in Marshall & Bell is a very good friend who has built up a great reputation within the secular recording world and regularly works with top recording artists. The first year of business has been exciting and challenging.

Then, after some extensive market research, it became apparent that the UK was lacking a vital area within the catering industry. Therefore I had to take action on this. After a week of intense intercession, fasting and poetry reading the idea came to me and "The Dog Ltd" was formed. Correct, I sell hot dogs for a living. The unique aspect of this venture is that we provide "Authentic American Hotdogs" served from a stainless steel New York street cart, just like you see in the movies! It's early days, but I think it could work. Franchise opportunities are available! Please visit www.ilovethedog.com.

One of the reasons for setting up the businesses was so that I could manage my time well and give more attention to music and the new band "Halfway There". I am the lead singer in the band and count it a great privilege to play with some of my closest friends. We have so much fun together. We recently played in the world famous "Cavern" in Liverpool where the Beatles used to play. Six bands played that night and, in all honesty, my Mum said we were by far the best! It is a great opportunity for me to write songs for a secular audience about my journey and about how we as a band believe that life needs to be lived to the full. Our dream is to be successful within the music industry and give all the glory back to the Giver of our talents. Please feel free to look at what we are up to at: www.myspace.com/halfwaythereuk.

Well, the end of this book is getting close. Thank you for taking the time out of your busy lives to read our story, it means a lot to us. It is hard to round up a story of this nature because it is still ongoing. Life to this present day is so precious and exciting. In the past, the thought of getting out of bed on a Monday morning would be a difficult one, but now I long for Monday mornings. I never want to go to bed early because I feel like I am missing out on life in some way. Every day is an exhilarating and stirring adventure for me. I go to the gym four to five times a week to keep fit and healthy. I do this because I believe that I have been given another chance at life and I need to make the most of it. I want to be an example to those who are in the midst of treatment, feeling that life will never be the same again, to show them that you can come out the other side better than when you started.

So, I've had mud in the eye. I would have favoured a faster solution, but I am writing this with good vision and a healthy body. I am one of the few that has been allowed to leave Neverland and I am determined to pay back as much as I am physically able. This book is part of that pay back.

In the words of a great friend of mine, "Don't tell God how big your mountain is, tell your mountain how big your God is."

In the final chapter my Dad will conclude the book.

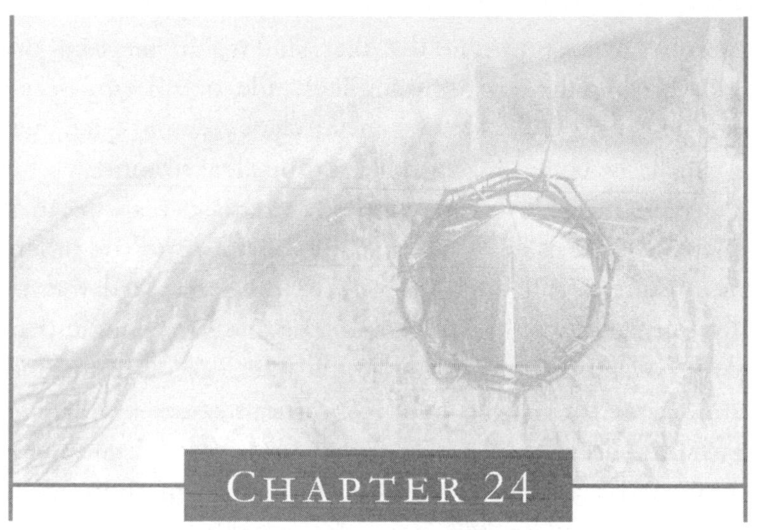

Chapter 24

Future Hope

Stuart

David's hair had grown back. It was not curly or ginger, two fervent requests that he made in his prayers. Life was beginning to turn back to normal. We had all in some ways taken a beating, but we were determined to live life in the future to the full. As another season changed in our lives blessings again began to flow. In fact, our family started to hope again.

Becki and Glen now have two children, Jermac and Trenton, which means that Irene and I have become Mama and Dada. It's an amazing feeling to be grandparents. Becki owns her own Stagecoach school, a theatre arts school, and continues to dance. I remember when she was a girl,

Norman Barnes prophesied that she would be seen on television, which has been fulfilled on a number of occasions. She leads dance at Grapevine each year and Glen, her husband, is the site manager. He is the ideal son-in-law.

Andrew continues to do well and last year became Primary Teacher of the Year, firstly for our region and then for the nation. In October last year we travelled to the London Palladium knowing he was in the finals, but at that point we didn't know he was the winner. You can imagine our excitement and the volume of Irene's screams when his name was announced as "Teacher of the Year". Irene, after years of back pain, is doing well and I am thoroughly enjoying life in New Life.

So back to David. After all he has been through he faces the future with a sense of deep gratitude. He involves himself in the life of the church, is on the worship team and is involved in youth work. Guitars still hang from the wall in his new home which he shares with the love of his life, Sarah. He loves to sing with "Half Way There" a band that are doing really well. He has written songs that express his faith and has chosen to live his life out loud. Following Leicester, for the first year David was provided with a well paid job. He was kindly offered a great opportunity as a trainee contracts manager with a London firm. This allowed him to get onto the housing ladder and drive a nice car. His life was beginning to change. He has now joined forces with Ben Marshall from Nottingham and "Marshall and Bell" a relatively new business has been birthed. You can find out about their activities on www.marshallandbell.com.

We have received an amazing amount of affirmation and support from so many of our friends. I don't know what we would have done had we not been a part of the Church.

During one of our phone calls with Jack and Trish Groblewski, Jack shared a picture with David. As he was praying he had seen a picture of an old Roman Soldier. His face was weather-beaten and showed evidence of many years of service. Over his eye Jack saw a scar and the words, "It was worth it". During a Good Friday showing of *The Passion of Christ* we were suddenly startled by the vivid image that invaded the screen. Jesus' face filled our sight. He had been whipped and viciously beaten. His right eye was swollen and closed. Irene and I grasped each other's hands and at the close of the film David came to us. He was very moved by the image. He knew that Jesus had taken his sins and that through His stripes healing was released. David's future would be wrapped up in the sacrificial finished work of Jesus. His future would be bright.

Though we are five years on I still have a daily routine as I pray for David's continued health. I guess I'll pray these words for the remainder of my days, though I'm not under any compulsion to do so. I include my daily prayer model hoping that this kind of approach will prove to be helpful to someone.

Daily prayer for David

> "I now place David under the covenant promises of the Lord Jesus Christ. I place the blood of Jesus over my dear son David; over his head, over his brain, over his eyes, over the orbital area of his eyes, over his neck and over his jaw. I place the blood of the Lord Jesus Christ, God's only Son, over his chest, over his heart and lungs, over his stomach and bowels, over his liver and kidneys. I place the blood of Jesus over his

abdomen, over his private parts, over his reproductive system, over his bladder, over his legs and over his feet and I declare from head to foot that no weapon forged against him shall prosper. I declare the finished work of Jesus Christ and by His wounds David is made whole. I claim the promise of Psalm 91 that he will dwell under the shadow of the Most High God, that he will be protected by angels, kept from falling and granted long life. In the name of Jesus Christ, the divine Son of God. Amen."

We now are about up to date with our story. If there are one or two who are afraid that we may have exaggerated, could I ask you to spend a few seconds looking at photographs in the centre of this book. They have not been doctored or filtered. You will see the real David then and now. I think you'll agree that you have a pretty remarkable visual aid to go alongside the picture we have attempted to paint in words.

In closing this book we end as we began with a dedication to the Miracle Maker. "God has saved the day and all will say my glorious." Our hope is that this story will carry His glory.

Appendix

Practical Advice for "Mountain Facers"

Some readers may be thinking, "Well, it's OK for you. As the pastor of a church you are in a privileged position to get help and support." That's true, we were very blessed, but potentially every church should want to engage with the needs of people. So here are a few practical suggestions:

- Don't keep your needs secret
- Don't try to go it alone
- Share your needs with your church leaders
- Ask your leaders to help you to put a plan together
- Take a positive attitude position
- Include people who will believe for breakthrough
- Stand firmly on the truth of the Scriptures
- Receive regular prayer
- Ask church leaders to anoint you with oil in accordance with the Word of God
- Don't avoid medical advice
- Don't read cancer stories in the newspapers
- Listen to worship CDs and good music
- Set short-term goals
- Ask God for personal scriptures and repeat them daily
- See yourself well and full of strength
- Give attention to diet and exercise
- Don't look up your condition on the Internet

We hope you enjoyed reading this New Wine book.
For details of other New Wine books
and a wide range of titles from other
Word and Spirit publishers visit our website:
www.newwineministries.co.uk
email: newwine@xalt.co.uk